The Complete Book
of
Canoeing and Kayaking

The Complete Book
of
Canoeing and Kayaking

Gordon Richards
with Paul Wade

Edited
by Ian Dear

B.T. BATSFORD LTD, LONDON

DEDICATION

To Chinzen
and
to all my other canoeing friends
of many nations but especially — in
no particular order — to:

Nicholas No. 2
Joachim
'King' P. Cole
JD
Jørn
Tor
Juan
Anatole
Vlado
RWE
Kewang
L.S. Stinker
Gonzalo
Andy
AV
Kjell
'S and F'

© Gordon Richards, Paul Wade and Ian Dear 1981
First published 1981

ISBN 0 7134 0761 1

Typeset by Tek-art Ltd, London SE20
and printed in Great Britain by
Robert Maclehose Ltd
Glasgow, Scotland
for the publishers
B.T. Batsford Ltd
4 Fitzhardinge Street
London W1H 0AH

CONTENTS

Foreword   6

Acknowledgement   7

Chapter   1   Introduction   9

Chapter   2   Canoes and Kayaks   13

Chapter   3   The Water and the Paddler   24

Chapter   4   Getting Started, the First Outing, and Care and Maintenance   38

Chapter   5   Safety, First Aid and Rescue   49

Chapter   6   Fitness for Competition   61

Chapter   7   Racing Competitions: Sprint, Slalom, Wild Water and Marathon   74

Chapter   8   The Role of the Coach in Competitions   96

Chapter   9   Other Canoe Sports: Sea, Surf, Polo, Sailing and North American Canoeing   100

Chapter 10   The International Scene and Interviews with Two Champions   115

Appendix   International Canoe Federation — Affiliated Members   127

Glossary   129

Index   141

FOREWORD

I am wholly committed in helping to promote kayaking and canoeing on a worldwide basis to anyone looking for fun, or for an escape from stress through relaxation coupled with physically demanding activity. I hope this book will prove to be a stimulus and a talking point to those already engaged in canoeing and kayaking as well as to those who want to become involved in what I have always believed to be the most exciting sport and recreation in the world.

Many books on kayaking and canoeing have been written, more often than not under the misleading generic term of 'canoeing', and the reader may wonder why I felt another was necessary. But my approach to the sport, with which I have been associated for many years as a participant, teacher/coach, administrator and promoter is, I feel, different in many respects from that of other authors on the subject. Within the sport and recreation of canoeing and kayaking there is a considerable diversity of individual disciplines and I have laid the emphasis of the book on those which have the greatest appeal to the greatest number of people, whether they be teenagers or octogenarians. I saw no point in devoting a large proportion of the book to the comparatively new — and wholly exciting — sport of surf canoeing when only a minute percentage of the many millions worldwide who go canoeing or kayaking for pleasure ever go near any surf. Equally, the recently introduced sport of canoe polo also has limited appeal at the moment, though hopefully it will expand rapidly, as it is capable of being introduced into many areas where natural water sources are at a premium.

On the other hand, marathon canoeing is gaining in popularity worldwide all the time whilst other disciplines such as slalom, sprint racing and wild water are retaining, and often increasing, their devotees, and I have therefore devoted a good deal of space to them. And as I strongly believe that one must get fit to practise a sport, and not merely use a sport to get fit, I have dwelt at some length on fitness and how to achieve it. I don't, nor would not, claim that this, or indeed any other parts, of the book are the definitive words on the subject but I hope they will act as a guide, a jumping-off place, as it were, for further research and activity.

Finally, both recreational and competitive kayaking and canoeing are technically exacting. To get the best out of your boat and yourself you need to know the latest techniques and understand how canoeing and kayaking have advanced during the last twenty years. I hope this book provides this information.

ACKNOWLEDGEMENT

My heartfelt thanks are due first to my wife, Mary; to my co-author, Paul Wade, and to his charming wife, Kathy, who held my hand both literally and metaphorically; to my invaluable secretary, Jane Mistri, whose patience never failed; and to Graham Mackereth of Pyranha Mouldings, who provided so much technical support as well as many of the photographs in this book. Without their help, support and guidance this book could not have been written.

Robin Belcher and Nigel Midgely gave me valuable advice on the surf canoeing and canoe polo sections, Ian Dear, who first approached me to write the book, has given me editorial guidance, while Graham Ingram-Monk has been more than generous with his time and photographs.

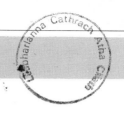

'Canoeing' is a general term that includes several different sports and several different craft. The basic similarity is that all use a small boat that is pointed at both ends, and propelled by paddles.

The craft commonly known as a 'canoe' had its origins in North America. The American Indians built a light wooden framework and covered this with birch-bark which was stitched firmly in place. Designed for use on lakes and rivers, it was usually about 20 feet long with a high bow and stern to negotiate rough water encountered when going over rapids. Wide in the beam for stability, these canoes had no deck and were usually propelled by two men, one fore, one aft, using single-bladed paddles. Both roomy and stable, these 'Canadian canoes', as they have come to be called, were able to carry heavy loads. Sensibly, when the French conquered parts of North America they used this native craft. Voyageurs and fur trappers used the rivers as we use roads today, as lines of communication from one settlement to the next, and their equivalent of the modern truck was a 35-foot long canoe.

Of course, the basic shape of the canoe was also used in other parts of the world. In South America, the Indians still hollow out a tree trunk as their ancestors did, by burning it away. In Lakeland, Florida, USA, a dug-out canoe was found in 1965

that was well over 19 feet long, 27 inches wide at the gunwale, 10½ inches deep with 2½ inch thick sides, it was carbon-dated as 3000 years old. Across in Africa and Asia the same technique was used, while in the Pacific, heavy canoes using an outrigger and several paddlers were the main means of transport between the islands. Local water conditions as well as local materials governed the design of the boats, which is why several paddlers were needed in the Pacific in order to burst through the huge waves that pounded the coral reefs. Even now, children in Australia use scrap material to build canoes. Mrs Joan Morison writes, 'Ever since the first time a small boy snitched a piece of old corrugated iron roofing — bent it — nailed pieces of fruit case or butter box in each end — sealed it with tar off the road — and took to the river with a packing-case paddle, the spirit of adventure has been with us.'

Meanwhile, in the frozen wastes of the Arctic, the Eskimos developed a different sort of boat to suit their needs in a harsh environment. Calling it a *kayak* (hunting boat), and its slower counterpart, an *umiak* (woman's boat), the Eskimo craft was not only low and narrow but also completely covered by a deck so that the paddler could sit inside the

1 North American Indian birch-bark canoe.

boat and keep dry and warm. He fitted snugly into a cockpit using the same greased sealskins that covered the boat to act as a waterproof 'skirt' or 'spray cover' around his waist. Because he and his craft were so watertight, the Eskimo hunter could be overturned by a wave or a seal and still right himself without having to get out of the boat. This manoeuvre, discovered much later by Europeans, was dubbed the 'Eskimo roll'. Because of the narrowness of a kayak, a double-bladed paddle was used so that the Eskimo could dip the blade into the water on either side of his craft.

The contrast between these early canoes and kayaks is considerable. Thanks mainly to modern materials and design, today's craft are brightly coloured and aerodynamically smooth; considerably stronger, yet lighter. From essential modes of transport, the canoe and kayak have developed into one of the cheapest and most popular forms of recreation available on water. Thousands of families go on holiday all over the world in Canadian canoes and kayaks, because these craft are not only able to be ridden anywhere but can be taken anywhere, too. Just as with other forms of transport, these have been developed for racing. Some racing is over short distances on still water (flat water racing), some is over longer distances down rivers and across lakes (marathon racing), while perhaps the most exciting is down foaming, rocky rivers (white water and slalom racing). The kayak has been put to use at the seashore, where surf canoeing is growing, and in swimming pools and on lakes, where canoe polo is popular. Canoes with sails have developed into slick racing machines that are rated as the fastest dinghies afloat. The canoe is also a valuable aid for lifeguards who patrol beaches.

However, the idea of using canoes purely for pleasure or sport is a recent innovation in a long history. In the middle of the last century the British were not only busy expanding their Empire, but also devoting a lot of their energy to sport. Eminent Victorians drew up rules and regulations for cricket and football, Rugby, athletics and swimming, even tennis and badminton.

Then came John MacGregor, a Scottish barrister. MacGregor was a great traveller and it was in North America and northern Russia that he saw the local people using canoes. In Britain, the clumsy rowing boat was used in day-to-day life, or else the expensive and technically complicated racing shell. The canoe seemed to be a simple and safe way of pottering about on the water.

He designed his first canoe in 1865, and got

2 John MacGregor, founder of the sport of canoeing in Great Britain.

Searles, Lambeth boatbuilders, to construct what he called a 'Rob Roy'. Not only was this designed to be propelled with a double-bladed paddle, there was also room for a small sail to be set in the centre of the canoe to take advantage of any wind. The 'Rob Roy' was heavy, about 90 pounds, and 15 feet long. A carefully constructed craft, clinker-built like a rowing boat, it contrasted directly with the Indian canoe with its light birch-bark walls, or the equally light and waterproof sealskin-covered kayak. Despite its disadvantages, MacGregor's canoe grew rapidly in popularity, thanks to the interest shown in it by the Prince of Wales and other members of 'high society'.

10

MacGregor's book *A Thousand Miles in the Rob Roy Canoe* was as popular as any adventure story of the day. Indeed, in 1866, the first-ever canoe club was formed at Richmond, on the River Thames just west of London. The following year a race, or regatta, was held with fifteen canoes taking part and when, in 1873, Queen Victoria gave the canoe club the accolade of being able to call itself the Royal Canoe Club, the sport's growth in Britain was assured.

The sport was soon picked up in North America, and the New York Canoe Club had already been established by 1871. Often canoeists were part of rowing clubs, and just as MacGregor popularized his invention by making romantic and daring trips along the rivers of Europe and the Holy Land, so in North America Nathaniel H. Bishop's trip from Quebec to the Gulf of Mexico did much to boost the appeal of what had become the North Americans' native craft — the open birch-bark Canadian canoe. His book *Voyage in a Papea Canoe* described his 2500-mile journey and was a great success when published in 1878. Once participants became adept at handling canoes, they wanted to show off their skills. The best way to do this was in water that was not flat and innocuous, but wild and bumpy. The sport became positively exciting as the canoeists discovered that they could shoot rapids and survive whirlpools. Racing, too, was popular and inevitably races were incorporated in rowing regattas.

However, it was not until the 1920s that the sport acquired a distinctly international flavour. Austria, Germany, Denmark and Sweden organized the IRK, the Internationaler Reprasentation fur Kanoesport. Czechoslovakia soon followed and by 1935 there were seventeen members.

The main reason for the growth of the sport was a new design of canoe. The German firm, Klepper, brought out a folding canvas canoe just before the First World War. This could be packed down into two rucksacks so that the cumbersome 'Rob Roy' was quickly outmoded. Canoeing became the favourite summer sport of many Scandinavians and Central Europeans.

Another important milestone was in 1927 when H.W. Pawlata of Austria demonstrated to his fellow-Europeans what Eskimos had known for centuries — the art of rolling a kayak. Bound in securely to their

3 The first 'Rob Roy'.

craft so that it was virtually part of them, Eskimos had devised a way in which to right themselves if they lost balance and rolled over so that they were head down in the water. Pawlata learnt about this technique from a sociologist called Rasmussen, perfected it himself and spread his knowledge. Until then people in kayaks who rolled over had had to free themselves underwater and then pull their boat to the shore, empty out the water and start again.

More and more expeditions were undertaken. In 1928 Captain Franz Romer crossed the Atlantic in 58 days. For his astonishing 3852-nautical-mile journey from Lisbon to St Thomas in the Caribbean he used a 19½-foot canvas kayak (folding canoe), and he averaged 56 miles a day. Between April 1936 and August 1937 Geoffrey Pope and Sheldon Taylor covered 7200 miles in a Canadian canoe fitted with a sail. They crossed North America from east to west, beginning in New York. Their route followed the Hudson River, Lake Champlain, and the St Lawrence River before going north across Manitoba. After wintering in Fort Chipewyan on Lake Athabasca, they went on to Alaska via Great Slave Lake, the McKenzie River, the Yukon and finally into Nome. Their longest portage (where they had to carry the canoe) was reputed to be a mere 14 miles!

The competitive side of canoeing grew up in 1936 when nineteen nations took part in flat water races at the Berlin Olympics. Canoes, kayaks and folding canoes with one or two paddlers raced in nine events from 1000 to 10,000 metres in length. At the same time, the recreational side of canoeing kept on growing. In Britain, canoeists formed a section of the Camping Club of Great Britain.

Another jump forward came in the early 1950s. Just as dressed skins had given way to canvas or wood, so canvas was superseded by PVC or plastic, and soon after, glassfibre (or plastic resin, GRP) made not only the construction of boats simpler and cheaper, but increased their longevity and repairability. Other less technical developments occurred in the 1950s. Instead of simply sitting in the bottom of his kayak Erik Seidel, the German champion, introduced a simple bag filled with sawdust to give himself a comfortable, more moulded seat. Knee grips and foot-rests were still not universally recognized. By the 1960s a lot more thought was being given to the design of boats. As the top competitors wanted faster, more efficient craft, so the ordinary paddler benefited from the innovative designs and materials which made canoes and kayaks tougher, lighter, and more stable — and at the same time faster and more manoeuvrable.

Throughout the modern era, Germany has been the mainspring of canoeing. There, the recreational side of the sport has flourished. At weekends thousands take part in training rallies. People 'race' in different classes (family, individual, junior, senior, veteran, etc.) over a given distance in a given time and small badges or stickers are awarded to those who finish inside the time limit. Incidentally, canoe touring in North America is also increasing steadily.

Canoeing depends on the availability of water, so different countries have different types of events. In Australia the races are long distance or touring races because the rivers there are long with uninterrupted navigation. In Austria, Germany and Czechoslovakia, there are mountain streams with 'big' water, so wild water racing is more popular. From that the more sophisticated slalom racing developed, based on the skiing tests executed on the same mountains in winter. In North America, the canoe rather than the kayak has developed as the racing craft. Again, long distance, flat or wild water racing are popular. In Britain, because of the diversity of water available, all branches of the sport have developed. Without a doubt, however, the strongest one competitively and recreationally is slalom, because the design of the boat is so stable that it lends itself to instant use without training, whereas the more sophisticated modern kayak is so finely balanced that it requires training and practice.

Ironically, the modern version of the sport is now being taken up in countries in Latin America and Asia which used native canoes centuries ago. However, the uniformity of modern sport demands that only internationally recognized classes of canoe and kayak are raced. At the same time there is no tradition of recreational sport in these countries, which makes the development of competitive canoeing more difficult. This is an aspect that still needs to be encouraged around the world, because the canoe and kayak are so versatile, able to handle anything from rough seas where they bob about safely like a cork, to flat water where they are ideal for simple exploration.

At present the sport's governing body, the International Canoe Federation, tends to look after competitions rather than preach the virtues of the canoe and kayak as a recreational vehicle. Sadly, too, the Olympics feature only flat water racing. Many countries, therefore, put their funds behind this less exciting branch of the sport at the expense of slalom or wild water racing. The future of canoeing will always lie in getting more people on to the water.

Canoes and kayaks come in all shapes and sizes. The overall length, the shape of the keel, the width of the boat all affect its performance in different water conditions.

The longer the craft is, the easier it will be to keep it running in a straight line, or 'track well' as canoeists say. At the same time, it is harder to turn. In order to make it more manoeuvrable, there has to be less boat in the water, so the banana-shaped keel is the answer. Canoeists refer to this curved keel as 'rocker', so the more rocker there is, the faster the boat can turn, although it loses speed.

The shape of the hull in the water is also important. A rounder belly gives the boat what canoeists call 'initial' stability which means that it will not turn over easily at first. The drawback, however, is that once they *do* tilt over a long way, they tend to capsize suddenly and flip back again. Therefore, many paddlers go for a craft that has a V-shaped hull that may be less stable initally but will not flip over suddenly when it does lean over. However, a sharp pointed V hull is strictly for racing experts as it has little resistance and topples the inexperienced straight into the water! .

Although a narrow canoe is less stable than a wider one, it is the 'cross-section' that governs performance. This dictates where the gunwale is — that is the point where the hull meets the deck. If the gunwale is low in the water, it usually means the bottom of the boat is flat and therefore difficult to roll. A boat with a higher gunwale will have lees initial stability but be easy to roll and therefore suited to wild water events.

There are two basic designs nowadays for the canoe and kayak. From these two craft several variations have been developed to deal with the innumerable types of water all over the world.

Canoes

Indian canoe

The North American Indian canoe was either a dug-out or the more common and famous birch-bark craft. Built with Stone Age tools from materials locally available, their design, size and appearance were varied so as to create boats suitable to the many and different requirements of their users. They were the most efficient craft for use in the wilderness, being propelled with a single-bladed paddel or pole. Paddlers could shoot small rapids and, as the boats were light, portage around larger obstacles. These canoes could be easily repaired without special tools and were used in varying conditions — from rapid streams to quiet waters and open lakes as well as the sea. Consequently, the size also varied from a one-man hunting and fishing

4 Traditional canoe (*G. Mackereth*).

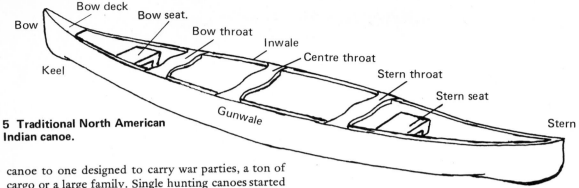

5 Traditional North American Indian canoe.

Labels: Bow, Bow deck, Bow seat, Bow throat, Inwale, Centre throat, Stern throat, Stern seat, Keel, Gunwale, Stern

canoe to one designed to carry war parties, a ton of cargo or a large family. Single hunting canoes started around 9 feet long and went up to 15 feet, whereas two-man craft were from 14 feet, with larger 'Voyageur' trading canoes as long as the 'Great Lakes 5½ fathom' canoes which exceeded 36 feet overall!

Touring Canadian canoe

At the end of the nineteenth century many manufacturers in North America started to produce canoes for leisure and expeditions. One of the largest and most famous was the Peterborough Company of Canada whose canoes were sold in Europe. European boat builders copied them – and called them 'Canadians' as opposed to 'Rob Roy' kayaks which they also built.

As many as 100,000 touring canoes are built in North America each year but in Europe they are only about 5 per cent of the more popular kayak market. They are usually 15 feet long for two people, with a beam of approximately 32 inches, though singles 12 feet long and four-man sailing versions 20 feet long are also available. While wood and canvas and aluminium are popular, new tougher materials such as Royalex are taking over.

The hulls are flat bottomed for stability as paddlers either use the seats or kneel. This produces a higher centre of gravity. When paddling hard in white water, canoeists kneel, pressing against the thwarts for control. Traditionally the ends are high, designed for large waves but more often now the ends, while still curving slightly upwards, are lower to reduce windage (wind resistance) as much as possible.

Canoes can be fitted with sails, engines, carry vast quantities of equipment, and though slower than a kayak because of their additional beam, really come into their own in versatility and comfort on an extended trip.

Sprint racing Canadian canoe

When these craft appeared at the 1976 Olympic

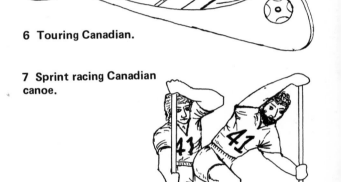

6 Touring Canadian.

7 Sprint racing Canadian canoe.

Games in Montreal, the Canadians could not understand why they were labelled 'Canadian canoes' as they bear no resemblance to the birch-bark canoes of North America. Since the boat came into the Olympics in 1936, it has become faster and sleeker, virtually a floating platform. The paddler kneels in what is a very unstable craft and powers his way up the course. Canadian canoes are raced as C1 and C2 at the Olympics but there are also C4s.

Down river racing Canadian canoe

Because of the rough water it encounters, this canoe has a special deck and spray covers for the paddlers. The bow is light to keep the nose from dipping, and in the double the two cockpits are slightly offset as one paddler works on one side and one on the other. The keel has a moderate rocker to allow both speed and manoeuvrability.

14

8 **A down river racing Canadian canoe in action** (*Colorsport*).

9 **Slalom Canadian canoe in action** (*Graham Ingram-Monk*).

Slalom Canadian canoe

This boat is paddled in a similar way to the down river racing Canadian canoe but the cockpits are slightly offset in the C2. With an accentuated banana-shape, the slalom Canadian can spin like a top as it negotiates the gates of a slalom course, since it is slightly shorter than the down river version.

War canoe

Popular in North America for inter-club competitions of a fairly light-hearted nature, the war canoe is often used to encourage youngsters to take up the sport. With room for nine paddlers, the boat is about 30 feet long, 3 feet wide and 17 inches deep amidships. Not surprisingly, it weighs about 120 pounds, because it is made of wood.

There is a marked growth of European interest in the war canoe because it generates a fascination amongst youngsters who, through its use as an introduction to canoeing, are being encouraged to take up the sport.

Kayaks

Sea kayak

Developed over many centuries by the inhabitants of the land of ice within the Arctic Circle, the best examples of the kayak come from the bays of Greenland. Built of driftwood and seal skin, the original craft form the basis of today's sea kayaks, known as 'Eskimos'. These are long and slender, designed originally for hunting and occasional transport. Now they are used for touring or expeditions. Made of reinforced plastics the craft vary between 16 and 19 feet in length and 19 and 24 inches in width. They have a long, fine clipper-like bow and stern with a shorter waterline length so that they rise and fall gently on waves. Flat bottoms keep them as stable as possible and their low decks offer little wind resistance, so they do not turn in side winds. Sea kayaks are often fitted with bailing pumps and watertight compartments with deck hatches for safety and storage of equipment.

Touring kayak

The touring kayaks vary enormously as different users look for different qualities, depending on the type of water they intend to paddle. They are usually flat-bottomed for stability, with well-rounded sides. The decks slope slightly in a moderate inverted V to help shed water. They are usually quite roomy in order to carry more equipment (for camping etc.) and the keel is fairly straight for a lake touring kayak and moderately rockered for white water touring. While lake boats have a fairly large cockpit for comfort and ease of loading, the white water tourer will have a slalom-sized cockpit for rolling and control in white water. A white water tourer averages 13 to 14 feet in length with a beam of 23 to 25 inches. A single lake tourer will be longer (14-16 feet) and wider (24-26 inches) and a double will be 15 to 18 feet long with a beam of 26 to 30 inches. The overall depth of both is between 11 to 13 inches.

Down river racing kayak

This is a single-seater which has a straight keel as it is designed for maximum speed in white water where it requires less turning ability than a slalom

10 Sea kayak.

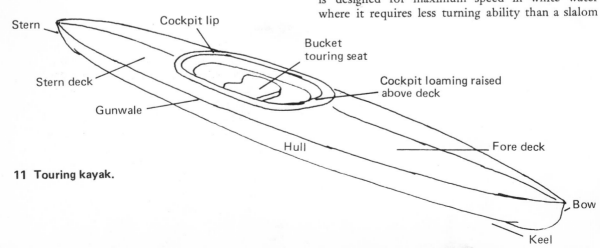

11 Touring kayak.

Stern

Cockpit lip

Bucket touring seat

Stern deck

Cockpit loaming raised above deck

Gunwale

Hull

Fore deck

Bow

Keel

kayak. Longer than the slalom K1, it is also less stable and often Sweden-formed, with a long nose and stubbier tail.

Slalom kayak

More effort and thought goes into the design of slalom kayaks than any other form of canoe or kayak. All craft have to combine instant manoeuvrability with speed, so that competitors can get in and out of gates in rough conditions and yet still maintain speed down the course. There is considerable keel rocker which means that the bow and stern actually stick out of the water, so that the minimum amount of boat is in contact with the water.

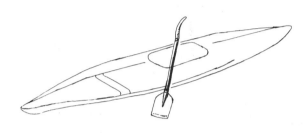

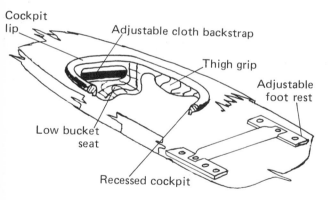

13 Cockpit of slalom kayak.

Sprint kayak

These kayaks are basically K1, K2 and K4.

Built for speed, there is no rocker on the keel and the hull is longer, lighter and narrower than other kayaks. A small rudder is operated by foot, and sprint kayaks are designed to be raced by one, two, or four competitors.

14 Sprint racing kayak.

Surf kayak

This is a cross between a surf board and a slalom kayak and is more suitable than either for intermediate sized waves. It not only enables the paddler to go out beyond the break line of the waves more quickly than on a surf board, but also gives a better run in than a slalom kayak. Made of reinforced plastic, it has the hull of a surf board with a buoyant bow and fine stern to give maximum control and to make rolling as easy as possible. It is quite short (between 9 and 11 feet long) with a narrow beam of 20 to 22 inches.

15 Surf kayak.

Surf ski

This is smaller in size and performance to a surf kayak but has less buoyancy and is therefore more difficult to paddle out through breakers. However, it is easier to move the body weight forwards and backwards to balance the craft and so it is becoming more popular. Held in by toe straps as well as knee and thigh grips, with a seat indentation, the paddler sits on, rather than in, a surf ski. The sizes are the same as for the surf kayak and construction is of reinforced plastic.

16 Surf ski.

BAT

The Baths Advanced Trainer was developed for use in swimming pools where the length of slalom kayaks would be a disadvantage. Being shorter, BATs turn quickly and are easier to control. With snub, rounded bows and sterns, no damage is done to the pool sides or to each other. Although a full-sized boat is paddled differently, all the basic strokes can be learnt with BATs, and in teams of five, canoe polo can be played with rules similar to water polo. Again reinforced plastic is used for construction.

General design characteristics

A craft with a pure semi-circular hull will always hold its position, in both flat and rough water even when the paddler leans over. It also has the minimum wetted surface area and is therefore very fast.

A craft with a flat hull and deck will always try to float base down, which is all right on flat water but unstable in rough water. This, however, is a very slow shape with a high wetted surface area, resembling a punt or barge, and if a wave breaks over the deck it will have a tendency to pull the craft over.

A craft which has fine ends (bow and stern) with a fairly straight keel will track well (run in a straight line). An example of this design is a K1 with an almost semi-circular hull. A rockered craft with broad, rounded ends will turn off a straight line easily but be controllable in transverse waves.

In general terms, therefore, a racing craft will be thin, almost semi-circular in central cross-section with fine ends and small rocker, and therefore unstable and slow to turn.

Touring craft on the other hand will be broader and round-sided with a flat bottom that produces more of a U shape. They will have more rocker but still keep an upright bow and stern to compromise speed and manoeuvrability.

A slalom or white water touring craft will be flatter on the bottom with very rounded sides. The ends will be highly rockered for extreme manoeuvrability, and rounded to give a flat cross-section that doesn't produce drag when turning, so that the craft can be turned against the flow of water.

Decks will vary in shape depending on whether the craft is to be used on flat water or rough water, if equipment is to be carried, what building material is used and whether when used on open water much windage is involved.

Smooth, semi-circular decks are generally the most efficient for moulded wood and RP craft flattening near the midships so that it is not too high. This deck shape is strong, does not easily catch the wind unless excessively high, and water flows off easily irrespective of the direction from which it hits the craft. In a white water kayak it is also a shape that is easy to roll.

Angled decks have to be used on canvas or plywood craft for economy and weight reasons. They are generally more susceptible to catching water when coming from the side but shed it faster when going head first into a wave. Their disadvantages outweigh their advantages and angled decks are a relic of the past on cheaply produced craft.

Flat decks are found on slalom and Eskimo craft, although usually comprised with a more rounded and more buoyant section in front of the cockpit both to shed water and to fit the paddler's body in. In the case of Eskimo craft, decks are flat to reduce wind effect. This can make the craft travel sideways with a beam wind and, if not balanced, will turn it into or out of the wind. In slalom craft the decks are flat both to reduce turning resistance and so that the craft can be 'sneaked' under the poles to save time and shorten the course.

Apart from BATs and surf kayaks, the normal minimum length of kayaks is 13 feet (4 metres). This usually produces a craft that will run fairly easily in a straight line but also has a fair degree of manoeuvrability. The amount of rockers, as previously explained, will greatly control manoeuvrability.

The longer the craft gets (depending on an equal amount of rocker) the more easily it will run straight. Touring singles and white water racers are usually about 15 feet (4.50 metres) in length, but Eskimo kayaks will exceed 19 feet (6 metres) although their actual waterline length is often short of this.

Slalom craft tend to be short as courses are

becoming increasingly tight and manoeuvrability is all-important. The novice tends to confuse increased 'beam' (width) with safety and this is often the opposite of reality. A beamy craft will often have a high degree of initial stability but this gives a false sense of security when in waves which will make the craft lean more easily, and the craft will soon be capsized. It is even more difficult to do an Eskimo roll or find support and strength to prevent it capsizing. It has other disadvantages, e.g. being slower.

Construction materials

The versatility of the different materials and constructions are both a great asset to the sport and a headache to the inexperienced. It is always preferable, therefore, to choose a well-known design and manufacturer and to seek expert advice.

ABS (acrylonitrile-butadiene-styrene) A vacuum moulded construction which can be brittle when cold. Available in many opaque colours, it is moderate-to-expensive and in single skin form very difficult to repair. In North America an ABS sandwich construction has been developed by Uniroyal of Indiana, whose Royalex consists of layers of cross-linked vinyl round solid ABS which in turn surrounds a foam core. The result has the look of fibreglass but it bouces off rocks like rubber, so it can even bend around rocks as well! Expensive but highly recommended; it is a rarity in Europe.

Aluminium canoes are durable and popular. Although they dent easily they are unlikely to split in normal use and can be repaired by re-rivetting. They have a cold feel and are noisy when knocked. Natural aluminium is the only colour and makes the craft expensive. They are mainly available in the USA and Canada.

Canvas is used to make wood canoes watertight, by stretching it over a plywood or bent wood frame with long wood stringers. Rigid frames are less expensive than folding designs. Canvas was always popular but has now been superseded by reinforced plastic and fibreglass which are lighter, less fragile and easier to build with.

Reinforced plastic (known as RP) and *fibreglass* (trade name for glass only). Less strong than polythene, ABS or aluminium, they are cheaper, more versatile in construction and more suited to small production runs. Available in opaque, translucent and dazzling sparkle finishes, RP is by far the most popular system of construction throughout the world.

Polythene This is a relatively new material in which kayaks are now being made by the rotationally moulded system. As with ABS there is a high capital investment with this system, so that it is only suitable for factory production. It does produce the toughest kayak yet built, but is only available in a limited number of designs and colours.

Wood Although this is still the most attractive material for building boats, it requires skill and a great deal of time, so wooden craft are generally expensive. Modern wood craft are built in three different ways. *Cold moulded veneer*: built by laying at least three layers of strips of veneer over each other at 45° to each other. The method is very slow and used only by the home craftsmen, but the craft are usually very beautiful when finished. *Cedar strip*: built of many ¾-inch strips of cedar strip pinned to a wood frame and then covered on both sides in RP cloth. This produces a light yet durable wood craft. *Hot moulded veneer*: only commercially made in Denmark and Sweden, these are generally recognized as the most beautiful boats of all. Especially popular as sprint racing craft, they are very, very expensive and delicate.

Plywood The cheapest form of wood construction, plywood boats are usually available only in kits to form a hard-chined shaped craft that is built up from panels of plywood sewn together and covered on both sides in glassfibre. The tops are reinforced with polyester resin. An easy kit to assemble that will produce an attractive craft but will not be as easy to maintain as RP.

17 Section of plywood canoe.

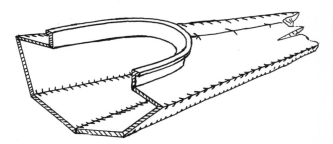

Bonding materials

Epoxy resin The most specialist resin of all, it is considerably tougher than other resins but is not commonly used because of the noxious fumes it gives off.

Polyester resin In its orthothalic form, it is the most commonly used building material today. It is relatively cheap, easy to use and is especially suitable for use with glassfibre. It is also available in the more expensive isopthalic form, which has better impact resistance and weathering properties.

Vinyl ester resin   This is used for the more expensive craft as its impact resistance and bond to kevlar are almost as good as epoxy resin but without the attendant health risks.

Reinforcements

Glassfibre   The most commonly used and cheapest reinforcement, glassfibre has been used for over 20 years and has a wide range of pigments and finishes. Easy to use, it is ideal for low-cost craft where impact and great stress are not of high importance. Glassfibre withstands a fairly high impact but breaks suddenly under great stress as it is inherently brittle.

Diolen   A polyester fabric which is used in conjunction with glassfibre to increase the impact resistance of the craft. It is a more flexible material that allows the laminate to sustain more damage before breaking.

Kevlar   An aramid fabric that has great resistance to impact, kevlar produces a light, yet strong craft. It is, however, very expensive and only suitable for use with vinyl ester resins or epoxy resins.

Carbon fibre   This is being accepted for craft used by national teams only slowly because it is phenomenally expensive. Only really suited to localized reinforcement because of its immense rigidity, it is even more brittle than all other materials.

Methods of construction

Hand lay-up

This, the most commonly used and cheapest method allows relatively easily custom-built craft to be made from all the above materials. The moulds used are usually in a three-piece set (hull, deck and seat) on to which a pigmented gel coat is sprayed or painted. This then gives a waterproof and cosmetic finishing layer. When this has 'cured' (set) the manufacturer will then back it up with layers of reinforcing materials to the specification of the order. The manufacturer's experience is very important as there are many small 'back-garden' businesses producing inexpensive craft from any mould they can cheaply buy or borrow, and from the cheapest low-grade materials.

The difference to the inexperienced eye is not apparent until compared with one of the better manufacturer's craft or until it has fallen apart!

The 'three mouldings' are fitted out with strengtheners bonded together, fitted with foot rests, end loops, seats and buoyancy to specifications and then after fully curing are ready for use.

Vacuum bag moulding

An American development, this method of building is only suited to craft that will have to endure very heavy stress, as it takes longer and uses more high-grade reinforcing materials. The craft will, however, last very much longer under stresses such as white water, touring and competition and therefore fully justifies the additional initial cost.

Paddles

Paddles are available in as wide a variety of constructions as are canoes and kayaks. Kayak paddles consist of two main parts, the shaft (or loom) and the blades. The canoe paddle has the handle and the blade. The shafts of both are available in three materials.

Alloy   Very strong and light, metal alloy has a cold feel unless covered in PVC.

RP   Very strong and light with little more whip than alloy or most wood shafts, RP has a better 'feel'. Usually only available in racing paddles because of its high price.

Wood   The traditional material is still the most versatile. If properly selected, wood is strong, light and has a good feel. The kayak paddle is usually oval in shape so that the paddler automatically rotates the feathered blade. This is important in white water or surf. The blades are also available in several materials and in several shapes.

18 Canoe blades.

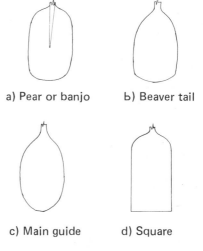

a) Pear or banjo   b) Beaver tail

c) Main guide   d) Square

19 Canoe handles.

a) Pear or palm

b) T grip

c) Canadian

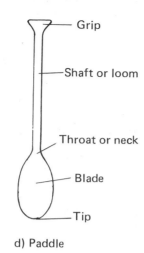

- Grip
- Shaft or loom
- Throat or neck
- Blade
- Tip

d) Paddle

20 Kayak blades.

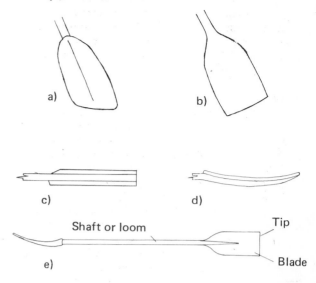

a)

b)

c)

d)

Shaft or loom — Tip

Blade

e)

Canoe blades and handles

For lake use the square blade is best as it pulls more water, but it is cumbersome in narrow channels where the narrower and more rounded blades become more useful, depending on the strength and personal preference of the user.

The grip is very important but still very much a matter of personal preference, although the T grip is most popular in competition and many tourers will use the pear grip.

Kayak blades

a) Asymmetric A racing blade that is designed so that both sides of the blade are equally immersed. By pulling the blade through the water there isn't a tendency for it to twist in the hand. This is often further aided by a rib running down the face of the blade.

b) Symmetric The more usual blade shape that is more suited for everyday use. Better with round tips rather than the old square tip designs, they are less likely to twist in the hands when catching submerged rocks.

c) Flat The most basic paddle that is suitable for complete beginners.

d) Curved or spooned A more advanced paddle with better performance. The curved blade grips the water better on entry and doesn't allow water to spill from the blade.

e) Kayak paddle with curved blade

Construction materials

ABS A popular modern material for blades that has largely overcome the problems of degrading in ultra-violet light. It makes a cheap rigid blade that wears well, though blades do suffer from chipping on impact.

RP Light and rigid, RP blades are available as a thin glassfibre blade which has a heavy rib up the back of the blade to give it rigidity. This is fine for straight paddling but gives turbulence and an awkward feel for other strokes, so they are often used as beginners blades or asymmetric racing blades. Framed RP is now being used for slalom paddles, which gets over the spined design disadvantage but these tend to wear on the tips unless protected. They are generally in the middle price bracket and increasing in popularity.

Wood Light, rigid and traditionally the cheapest in kit paddle form or most expensive in the hand-laminated and finished form, wood paddles are certainly the most beautiful. If carefully selected they are a good investment as the feel of a good wood paddle cannot be matched in any other material.

Other equipment

Spray decks/spray covers/spray sheets

A spray cover has a heavy elastic all round the edge, designed to grip underneath the lip of the cockpit. It is easiest to put it on round the waist while still on dry land. Then once the paddler has settled into the kayak, he or she just leans back and fits it around the back of the cockpit. Then, still leaning back, he stretches the front of the spray deck over the

21 Spray cover.

is to have a series of four or five wood, plastic or aluminium rests along the side of the boat so that the paddler can select whichever feels more comfortable. These are 2 or 3 inches square. The alternative is a bar that goes across the boat, but until the beginner is experienced this may need adjusting, and groping around in the innards of a boat is always difficult, so the series of rests is the easiest.

The rudder

The rudder is hung on the stern of the craft and usually enables the blade to lift if it hits an obstacle. Used for inland touring and marathon racing.

The understern is a more efficient rudder system that is only suitable for deep water racing or touring.

The tiller bar is pivoted in front of the foot rest and by pushing it with your feet you can turn the craft.

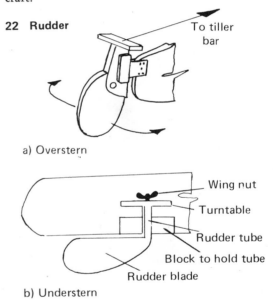

22 Rudder
To tiller bar

a) Overstern

Wing nut
Turntable
Rudder tube
Block to hold tube
Rudder blade

b) Understern

front of the cockpit and, holding it firmly there, feeds one side round, then the other. Spray covers are usually made of nylon, and the tension between the paddler's waist and the cockpit ensures that the water runs off. More advanced covers are made of neoprene which is a softer, less durable material, but provides a better seal and is warmer round the stomach. Top competitors and rugged explorers always use it.

Before setting off, paddlers should check that the elastic is tucked well in below the combing grip, especially at the back. There is no point in being in full flight only to have the spray cover pop off!

Foot rests

These are very important in a kayak, as the whole body is braced against the seat and foot rests. These must never hold the feet in. In case of an accident, the feet must always be able to slip out immediately. At the same time, the paddler might be jarred forward suddenly so the feet and legs must not be able to slide down the boat and get stuck. There have been accidents because paddlers have used a flat plate of fibreglass as a foot rest. On impact these have pivoted, letting the feet shoot past which have not been able to be withdrawn again. The best idea

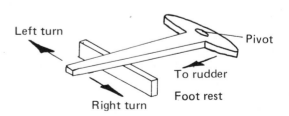

Left turn
Pivot
To rudder
Foot rest
Right turn

23 Tiller bar.

TYPES OF CRAFT

PADDLER'S SIZE		SLALOM				WILD WATER RACING				SPRINT + MARATHON				TOURING							
		KAYAK		CANOE		KAYAK		CANOE		KAYAK		CANOE		KAYAK SINGLE		KAYAK DOUBLE		CANOE BOWMAN		CANOE STERNMAN	
IMPERIAL	METRIC	IMP	MET	IMP	MET	IMP	MET	IMP	MET	IMP	MET	IMP	MET	IMP	MET	IMP	MET	IMP	MET	IMP	MET
Under 5'2"	157	6'6"	200	4'7"	140	7'0"	212	4'11"	150	7'1"	216	5'1"	154	6'9"	206	7'2"	220	4'11"	150	5'1"	154
5'2"-5'4"	157-163	6'7½"	202	4'8"	142	7'0"	214	5'0"	153	7'1"	216	5'2"	158	6'10"	208	7'3"	222	5'0"	153	5'2"	158
5'4"-5'6"	163-168	6'8½"	204	4'9"	146	7'1"	216	5'1"	156	7'1"	216	5'4"	162	6'10"	208	7'4"	224	5'1"	156	5'4"	162
5'6"-5'8"	168-173	6'9"	206	4'10"	148	7'1"	216	5'2"	158	7'2"	218	5'5½"	166	6'11"	210	7'4"	224	5'2"	158	5'5½"	166
5'8"-5'10"	173-178	6'10"	208	4'11"	150	7'2"	218	5'3"	160	7'2"	220	5'7"	170	6'11"	210	7'5"	226	5'3"	160	5'7"	170
5'10"-6'0"	178-183	6'10"	208	5'0"	152	7'2½"	220	5'4"	162	7'3½"	222	5'9"	175	6'11½"	212	7'5"	226	5'4"	162	5'9"	175
6'0"-6'2"	183-188	6'11"	210	5'1"	154	7'3½"	222	5'4½"	164	7'3½"	222	5'11"	180	6'11½"	212	7'6"	228	5'4½"	164	5'11"	180
over 6'2"	188+	7'0"+	212+	5'2"+	156+	7'3½"+	222+	5'5"+	165+	7'4"+	224+	6'0"+	184+	7'0"+	214+	7'6½"+	230+	5'5"+	165+	6'0"+	184+

It should be noted that these are only basic guides and that really it is very much personal preference that should be your guide when you have had some experience. Stronger paddlers may wish to have one size larger than that specified for their height whilst weaker than average men or girls may wish to have one size shorter.

CHAPTER 3

The Water and the Paddler

Understanding the water

It is possible to predict reasonably accurately the behaviour of flowing water in a natural environment. This facility which paddlers call the ability to 'read' water is of utmost importance to both the recreational and the competitive paddler and is essentially one of the basic skills. A paddler who can read a river will always beat a stronger competitor who cannot.

Currents flow at different speeds in different parts of the river. In a smooth river the current is strongest in the middle and on, or near, the surface. As there is friction resistance against the banks the current is slower there and, in fact, water can flow upstream — almost like a separate body of water. So, going downstream the paddler tries to stay in the middle of the river and going upstream, he keeps to the sides.

24 Speed of water.

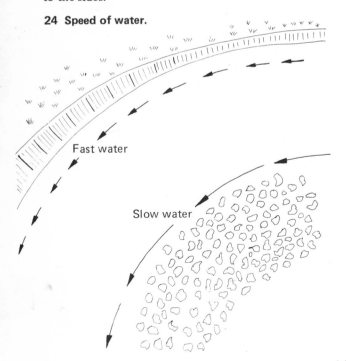

Fast water

Slow water

25 Eddies caused by rocks.

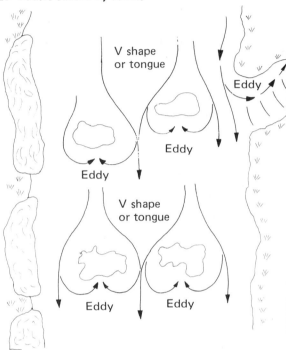

V shape or tongue

Eddy

Eddy

Eddy

V shape or tongue

Eddy

Eddy

Where a river bends, the fastest water will be pushed to the outside while the slower water flows along the inside of the curve. Acting like the centrifugal force of a wheel, the faster water cuts away at the bank and that is where the canoeist often encounters trees hanging low over the water. Here the faster channel can also be the most dangerous.

Paddlers must recognize and follow the main passage. On a quiet stretch of water this is down the centre of the river where the water is uniformly deep. However, on approaching turbulent water a V in the river's flow signposts the way to a deeper section of the river. Turbulence or white water looks exciting because air has been sucked into the water and then it froths up. This foam provides less buoyancy to a canoe or kayak, while darker water (with no air bubbles) is a 'solid' base for paddling. Fig. 25 shows a line of rocks in the middle of the river. As the faster water rushes round the rocks it stirs up the quiet water at the sides of the main channel, to form a backwash or eddy. This water appears to be moving back upstream and can be used as a resting place to check out the rest of the rapid and, if necessary, to pull the boat up on the bank before going to inspect the river just below.

It is also worth remembering that behind any large rock is a small eddy which can hold the boat while the paddler takes a rest. An eddy does not have to be at the side of the river — any rock will have a certain amount of water pouring upstream behind it. When resting in an eddy, the paddler should make sure that the bow is not caught by the fast main current coming round either side of the rock or else he will be whisked off downstream again! As the paddler has to follow the main stream using the biggest V in a rocky river he should try to plot his route ahead of time by inspecting it from the bank to get a good 'feel' for where he is going — just like reading a road map.

When water bounces off a firm shore made of rock or concrete, it often reappears a few feet away from the shore bubbling up in a way that is confusing to novices. This is known as 'reflection slope'. As well as the banks or big rocks affecting river flow, any irregularities in the bed of the river throw up different currents. A common one is is a 'stopper' which again has the effect of reversing the current and literally stops any canoe or kayak that hits it, as fig. 26 demonstrates.

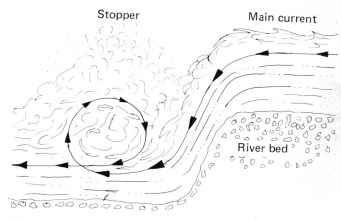

26 A stopper.

Rapids are generally formed by a restriction in the flow of the river as shown in fig. 27. This could be when it reaches a narrow gorge or even broad shallows. Shallows occur in rivers which flow down flat valleys and are caused by deposits of rock and soil that the river has gouged out upstream and dropped further downstream. Shallows may also be found at curves and at junctions with other streams which have brought down their own deposits. They often have sand bars in them and in a broad river these can present a confusing choice of channels. This type of rapid often becomes so shallow that the canoeist cannot paddle any further and has to get out and either carry the boat, or allow it to float downstream as he walks it down on a rope. This is known as 'lining down'.

27 Formation of rapids.

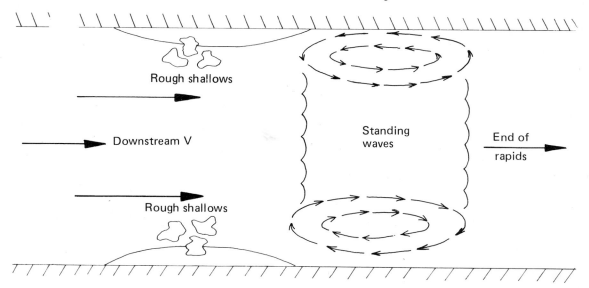

Wild mountain streams are obviously steeper in gradient and produce more forceful rapids around 'boulder fields' or 'rock gardens'. Similar in many ways to the rapid, but on a much grander scale, the large rocks that tumble down the bed of a river can form self-supporting barriers which tend to pile up until dislodged by a flood. Boulder gardens in low water are often unnavigable but in high water they provide an exciting paddle.

Rivers can fall into gorges or canyons which are particularly difficult for the paddler to reconnoitre. The novice should steer well away from these unless he is part of an experienced group who know his capabilities, are familiar with the river and are sure that the one can handle the other. These features in the river are usually caused by a broad river going into a narrow canyon and, if escape routes are not known, it is advisable to walk out safely before the situation becomes too difficult. Awe-inspiring and frightening to the inexperienced, canyons often have 'ledges' which are exposed geological formations that have resisted the wear the river has given to the rest of the rock bed and have remained 'upstanding' by comparison. These ledges are often found at the ends of deep pools from where they descend in a sort of staircase down to another pool. These often collect boulders and can be hard to distinguish in rock gardens. Some ledges are not unlike weirs and dams and, occurring in a series of steps, they may cause a paddler to change direction, creating a very complicated descent.

Man-made obstructions such as dams, weirs and fish traps are potentially dangerous because the last person the engineers and planners consider is the canoeist. Man-made obstructions are usually more angular and regular than those of nature. Dams usually drop water into relatively still pools and the result is often a dangerous underwater stopper or a 'tow back' below the dam's lip. These often occur in a straight line across the river and once caught, there is no escape for the paddler. A careful inspection will often reveal logs, tin cans, polythene bottles, all trapped and rolling round and round and going nowhere. The same could happen to the paddler, so the motto is 'stay clear!'

Sometimes the weir may be V shaped or have a nick in it, creating a strong shoot of water or possibly a fish ladder. In good conditions it is possible to shoot the weir in safety but this should never be attempted without having experienced paddlers on hand who have done it before and are sure of the novice's ability.

If, in spite of being careful, a paddler gets caught up in one of these, the only remedy is to swim out underneath the stopper. This can be done if he removes his buoyancy aid, gets rid of the boat, spray cover and paddles and then swims strongly down and out underneath the stopper, surfacing as soon as possible. Obviously, allowance has not been made for the tow back but the most important thing is not to panic. The paddler should also look out for spikes in wooden dams as well as old iron reinforcing bars in concrete dams, which may be hidden underneath the surface.

However, when looking at currents in a river, a canoeist should always be aware that those are only the currents on the surface. Underneath there can be vicious cross-currents which are quite impossible to fathom. These can be very dangerous in the simplest looking situation. In rapids they get even more complex and these underwater currents manifest themselves in 'whirlpools' and in 'boils'. The whirlpool is the downwards sucking of water which from the surface looks like water going down a plughole, circling round anti-clockwise before dragging any objects down into the river and sweeping them downstream.

A 'boil' is almost the opposite, where an underwater current comes up, often at the bottom of gorges and rapids where currents become disturbed and irregular. They will often appear as a huge boiling mass of water coming up from the riverbed often moving up and down in height. These should be avoided at all costs as they tend to suck the paddles out of a canoeist's hands as well as throw his boat violently about.

Three techniques used in flowing water

Ferry glide This is a clever way of making the current do the work. Used to go across a river without going down it, the ferry glide is most useful to go sideways when confronted by an impenetrable barrier of rocks or dangerous waves.

The paddler should always lean downstream executing the ferry glide, with the bow of his craft pointing up *into* the current. The idea is to paddle forwards on one or both sides to negate the current as the boat drifts slowly across. Done well, the paddler will need little effort and will save considerable time manoeuvring. The angle of the bow to the current will alter the speed at which the canoe or kayak moves. A reverse ferry glide is harder to execute as the paddler cannot see the variations in the strength of the current. He still leans downstream, but has to glance over his shoulder to check the water.

28 Ferry glide.

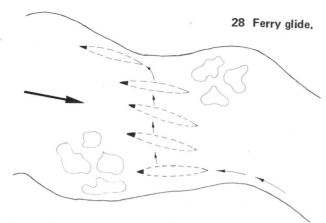

The current can also be used to turn a canoe or kayak, simply by sticking the bows into the mainstream. The paddler does not always have to use a paddle stroke.

29 Breaking in and breaking out.

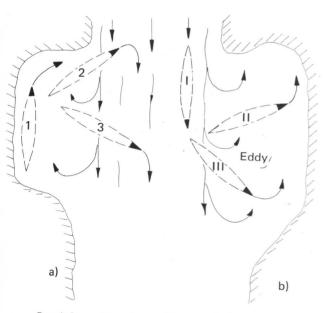

Break-in and break-out These techniques are used all the time by slalom and white water paddlers. Again, the idea is to get the water to do the work, especially in eddies.

a) Boat 'resting' in eddy, bow pointing upstream, wants to 'break in' to the mainstream again. By paddling forward and getting the front third of the boat into the mainstream, it will quickly be turned by the current. A low telemark turn on the downstream side helps it round.

b) In order to have a rest, a paddler coming downstream 'breaks out' of the main current into an eddy by turning sharply using a forward sweep stroke to force the front third of the boat into the eddy. As it enters the eddy, the bow swings upstream while the stern of the boat is pulled downstream. A low telemark on the upstream side completes the turn into the peace of the eddy.

30 British team gold medallist, Richard Fox, in a break-out sequence at Bala, north Wales, 1980 (*G. Mackereth*). *Continued overleaf.*

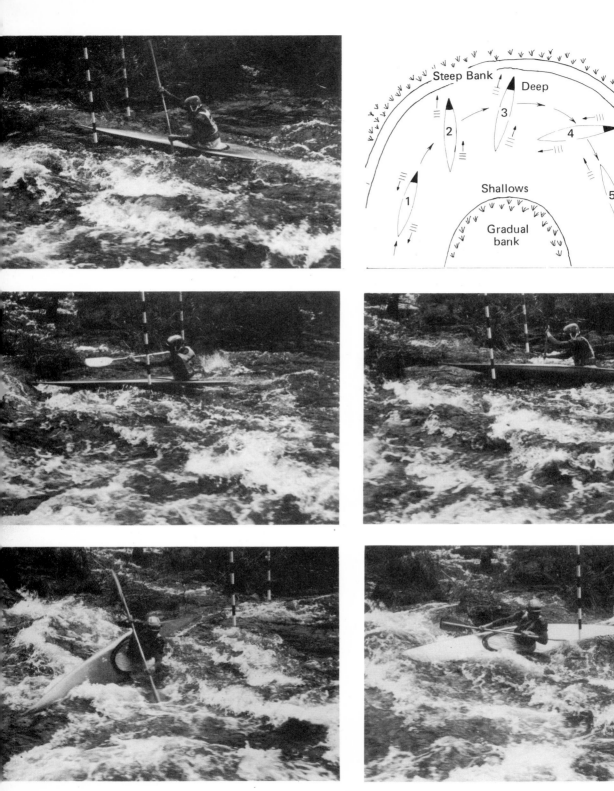

31 Using the technique of 'breaking in' to go round a bend. Note that the paddler does not take the obvious line, but lets the faster current do the work.

Paddling strokes

Although it is always best to learn from a coach or competent club mates, a book can act as memory jogger, so that the reader can practise on his own. All strokes and techniques can be used both forwards and backwards, and both from left and right. By altering the angle of the shaft and the blade as well as its proximity to the kayak, a stroke can have a different effect. Placing the blade well forward or back, leaning the craft over — even executing the stroke slowly or quickly — all change the effect. Therefore practice will let the paddler know when to use the right stroke.

What to do in a kayak

Once in the kayak, the novice picks up the paddle making sure that the paddle is right or left 'control' depending upon whether he or she is right- or left-handed. The right-hander uses his right to grip the paddle, while the left allows the paddle to rotate. It is handy to mark the right place to put the hands on the paddle, so the grip is correct.

Forward paddling The paddler should sit upright in the boat with his body as relaxed as possible. His shoulders should be relaxed too, though he should keep his head up, looking straight ahead. As soon as he looks down at his cockpit or at the bow of the kayak, he will only start to worry and, in any case, this position, looking down, makes breathing more difficult.

Paddling is not merely an arm-action. It uses the muscles of the shoulders and the back too. As the hip muscles are amongst the strongest in the body, these come into play as well. The hips should show just above the coaming of the cockpit, so the paddler's seat should be adjusted accordingly, and kept horizontal, not tilted forward.

The position of the legs is important, as they help to stabilize the craft. Legs should always feel comfortable and are best kept together at the knees and heels with the toes pointing outwards. The paddler will find that his legs are most comfortable when the knees are slightly bent. If they are stretched too straight or bent up too high, they will be uncomfortable after a short while.

The hip comes into play as soon as the paddler

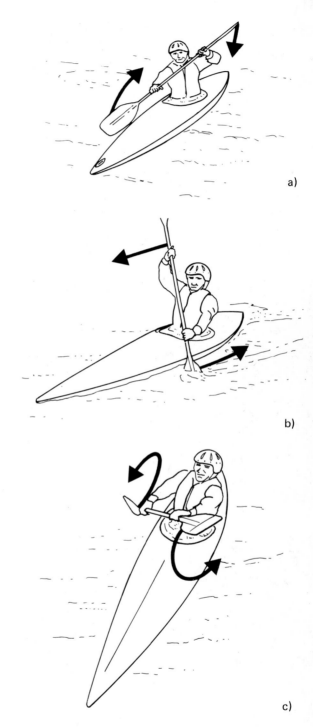

32 Forward paddle stroke **a)** Start of stroke **b)** With blade in water, bottom hand pulls, top hand pushes **c)** Finish of stroke.

makes his first stroke. As soon as the hip moves forward, so too does the shoulder. The hand then moves the paddle forward at about nose level, but must go straight forward, not across the line of the boat. The elbows are kept as low and relaxed as possible, as the art of paddling does not require massive strength but rather rhythmical movement. The paddler should not lean the trunk of his body forwards or backwards to try to increase the length of power of his stroke.

The arms are kept low, as this is a stable, comfortable position and also gives more turning power. The right arm pushes forward as far as it can go, then the paddle is dipped into the water vertically about 1 foot from the side of the kayak. As the right arm pulls back, so the left arm pushes forward. The right hand acts as a pivot throughout this pulling/pushing action as the blade travels parallel to the boat. As the left arm is fully extended forward, so the blade can come out of the water, level with the hip. This is where the tricky part comes in.

The right wrist is dropped, which automatically rotates the shaft of the paddle in the palm of the left hand. This means that the blade on the left-hand paddle is ready to present a full face to the water on the next stroke.

The rest of the sequence is a repeat, as the left arm pushes forward, dips the blade into the water about 1 foot from the boat, and the right arm pushes forward using the left-hand as a pivot!

When this stroke is completed, the right wrist is again dropped so that the paddle rotates back ready for the next stroke. This is, however, a *continuous* action, without a pause between strokes.

Throughout the paddling, the novice should be as relaxed as possible, paddling *slowly*. No great effort is needed. When the arms are pushed forward they should not cross the centre line of the course, and the same effort should be made on either side. If the canoe goes off course, then a couple of extra strokes to the right (to turn left) or to the left (in order to turn right) brings the paddler back on course. In order to stay on course, it often helps to aim for a stationary object like a tree or a post.

Reverse paddling Once this simple skill has been learnt, the idea of stopping or even going backwards is possible by reversing the normal strokes. However, the paddle is still held in the same way — *the blade is not turned round*. The paddler should always glance behind to ensure that he is not going to run into someone or something, then again using the hand as a pivot he reverse paddles using the push/pull motion of the arms.

33 Reverse paddle stroke using back of blade.

To stop a kayak as it goes forward requires an equal number of sharp reverse strokes on each side of the craft, ensuring that the paddle is clear of the sides. Any abrupt stroke close to the sides can induce a capsize, especially if the paddler digs down too deep in the water.

These are the simplest strokes and take time to perfect. Many more strokes have been devised to turn and control the kayak in currents and rough water. They have all developed because the kayak is so light that it becomes virtually part of the paddler's body, like a mermaid's tail! It is therefore possible to lean the kayak on its side without capsizing, bending from the waist.

Bow sweep stroke This is an easier way of turning the kayak, or indeed correcting its course. The paddler reaches further forward by twisting at the waist, and instead of pulling the blade straight back parallel to the boat he sweeps it round in a semi-circle, keeping it submerged just below the surface. The paddler should make the arc as big as possible, bringing the blade right to the back of his craft and allowing the kayak to lean over slightly. This means there is less boat in the water, so it is easier to turn.

Reverse sweep stroke This is simply the reverse of the forward sweep stroke and, as with *all* kayak strokes, the blade is never reversed. The sweep starts as far back as possible, near the stern of the boat. The paddler leans into the paddle and sweeps it in an arc up to the bow of the boat. He may need more than one sweep in either direction to turn the boat. He will also realize after a while that the angle of the blade in the water affects the stroke. If the top edge is angled slightly so that it is the leaning edge, then the paddler will be able to put more weight on the paddle and get a quicker response from the

34 Bow sweep stroke.

a) Start of stroke.

b) Boat is turning.

35 Draw stroke.

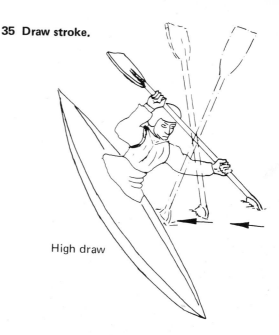

High draw

36 Slap support stroke.

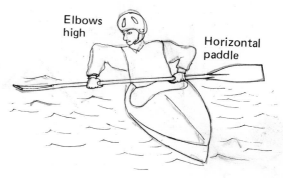

Elbows high

Horizontal paddle

a) Start of stroke.

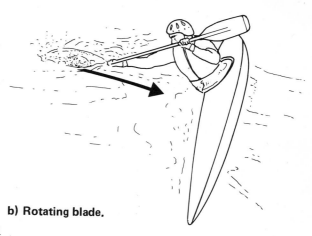

b) Rotating blade.

stroke. Eventually, he will use his skill when 'sculling for support'.

Draw stroke Used to draw or move the kayak sideways, the paddle is held in the usual way but planted in the water level with the cockpit and a couple of feet away from the boat. With the top hand at or above head height and the bottom hand again acting as a pivot, the paddle is pulled towards the kayak. The top hand tends to push outwards as the blade pivots about the lower hand. The effect is for the kayak to move *towards* the blade. As soon as the blade is near the boat, the paddle is rotated so that it is sideways on and can be lifted out of the water. If the paddler leans outwards he gets a longer stroke, but he should not pull too hard or deep, or especially *too close*, in order to avoid capsizing.

By placing the paddle forward of the cockpit, the bow will turn; to the rear of the cockpit and the stern turns!

Slap support This is a badly named stroke, as slapping a blade down on the water is the last thing needed. However, that is the standard name. The paddler actually presses the flat blade of his paddle

31

firmly down on to the surface of the water, about 2 feet from the kayak. The hands should hold the shaft in the usual place, as the paddler feels the support that the water can give. A quick rotation of the blade and it can be lifted out of the water and slapped or pressed down again. The paddler can use the support the blade gives to lean on to the paddle and should lean further and further each time until the elbow, then the shoulder and eventually the head touch the water. The idea of this is to practise for more advanced strokes and to get the paddler used to the 'feel' of the water and the way in which he can use it to his advantage. Naturally, he needs to have a spray cover fitted properly beforehand! Practising the slap support from side to side regaining the upright position also brings the hips into play. The hip-flick is important in kayaking as it helps control the stability of the boat.

Sculling for support A continuation of the slap support and the sweep, in sculling for support the paddle blade is used to sweep back and forwards

38 Stern rudder stroke.

when they are being carried along by the wind, current or in surf. The paddle is held in the usual way and placed parallel to the side of the boat with the blade dipped in the water. To make a long run to the left, the left-hand blade is trailed in the water; the right-hand blade is used to move to the right. More movement can be obtained by pushing the paddle outwards, using the back of the blade against the current.

The canoe can also be controlled by using the opposite stroke, the bow rudder.

Low telemark turn This is used for quick turns or fast flowing rivers, but should be practised beforehand on still water. Like so many more advanced strokes, it requires a certain amount of lean. The blade is jabbed into the water behind the paddler (to his right to turn right, to the left to turn left) as for the stern rudder and is used as a pivot as the speed of the water moves the kayak round. At the same time, the full body weight of the paddler is put on the paddle which is pushed forward by the lower hand as in the reverse sweep stroke.

Paddling strokes are never used individually but rather in a sequence. Paddlers tend to build up patterns of their favourite strokes which link together so that turns are carried out as quickly and efficiently as possible. They have to become automatic, or else they will be executed too late!

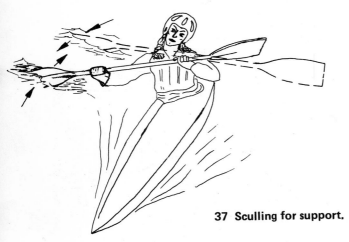

37 Sculling for support.

just below the surface of the water. The secret is to angle the blade at about 30° and then to rotate the paddles on the reverse move. The paddler practises leaning over further and further until the body is totally immersed and the bottom of the kayak is exposed. Properly executed, this will make the learning of the Eskimo roll very much easier.

Stern rudder It took man centuries to come up with the idea of using a rudder, placed at the stern of a ship. The original steering method was to have a huge oar or board at the side of the ship. Called a steer-board, this is how we derived the word 'starboard' as this device was always on the right-hand side of the boat. Kayakers use the same technique

39 Low telemark turn.

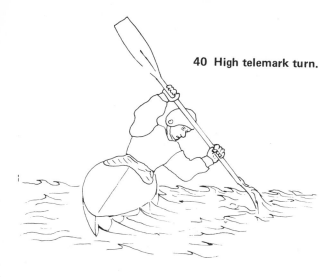

40 High telemark turn.

High telemark turn This is often used for a break-out as the paddle acts as a firm pivot for the fast-moving kayak to turn on. After a forward sweep stroke and holding the paddle in the normal paddling position, the paddler raises his arms head high with both elbows pushed forward. The blade is pushed into the still water in the eddy and the paddler leans in hard with the paddle almost vertical. The kayak turns sharply into the eddy.

Racing stroke Competitors in flat water racing need a perfect forward paddling stroke. Any slight faults are exaggerated when a paddler goes flat out, and the result is a slower performance than the output of energy deserves.

a) The dip of the left blade is just in front of the bow wave, the body is fully rotated with left arm straight so that the blade can be put in the water as far forward as is possible. Right elbow is kept low with right hand reaching forward at about eye level.

b) The end of the pulling phase on the left side with body having rotated fully and the arm having bent at the elbow. The right arm is relaxed, but becoming straight. The left foot is pushing on the foot rest to assist in the rotation of the body.

41 The racing stroke.
Continued overleaf.

c) The right arm becomes fully extended at shoulder level as the left blade 'jumps' from the water. The body is fully rotated for the stroke on the right to begin.

d) The right shoulder is dipped as the blade enters the water. Left wrist is 'cocked' backwards so that the right blade is ready to commence the stroke.

e) Body is half way through the rotation. The arm has started to bend at the elbow. Right foot pressing on the foot rest to assist rotation.

f) Bad technique is demonstrated in this photograph. The left arm and hand have crossed the centre line of the boat too much, hence the right blade is recovered from the water too far from the side of the canoe. Good rotation with the right foot pressing on the foot rest to assist the rotation.

A coach needs to observe every movement to ensure that no faults have crept into the technique. He should, along with the paddler, check that the height of the seat is correct (hips above coaming) and that the paddle is not lifted above eye level, which is also inefficient. He should ensure that the body rotates from the hips and shoulders and is not rolling enthusiastically from side to side. The knees can sometimes be kept too high as the paddler imagines that he is getting a better grip. He is merely constricting his movements. Another fault is the notion that the longer the paddle is in the water, the better and more powerful the stroke. Once the blade passes the paddler's body it is coming out of the water, travelling vertically and *lifting* water rather than pulling it — again, wasted effort. The path of the blade should always be parallel to the craft, which in turn should be going straight up the course. Any curves in the paddle stroke are hindering the straightforward motion of the boat. The blade itself should always be at 90° to the kayak, presenting the full face to the water for maximum effect.

What to do in a canoe

Unlike the kayak, the canoe comes in more varieties —

from the big, open Canadian canoe to the Olympic-style craft. Some paddlers sit, others stand, many kneel. Whatever position is adopted, the basic strokes are the same.

42 Paddling positions.

a) Sitting.

b) Kneeling.

43 Forward paddle stroke.

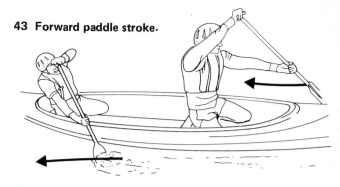

a) Start of stroke.

b) Paddles fully immersed.

c) End of stroke.

Forward or bow stroke The correct grip for the Canadian paddle is with one hand on the grip (at shoulder level) and the lower hand at slightly less than 90° from it down the shaft, about a shoulder width apart. Unlike the kayaker, the canoeist bends well forward at the waist when dipping the blade in the water, as far forward as possible. The paddle is kept as vertical as possible, pulling through parallel to the side of the craft, with the blade at right angles to 'grab' as much water as possible. The top hand pushes forward as the lower arm pulls. The bow is pulled over sideways to balance the one-sided impetus from the single blade.

Paddlers in C2s should practise paddling in both the bow and stern positions to appreciate the dif-ferent reactions of the canoe. As the blade should be properly immersed, novices should make sure that the shaft is not too long for their purposes. The hand at the top of the paddle is the one that grips firmly and pushes while the lower hand acts as the guide. In order to get the paddle forward for the next stroke, it is kept low and feathered, moving low over the water.

Backwater stroke This is the reverse of the above, used to reverse or stop.

Bow sweep This is the same as the kayaker's for-ward sweep as the paddler places his paddle in the water as far forward as he can and then sweeps the

a)

b)

**44 Bow sweep stroke a) Start of stroke
b) Finish of stroke.**

about 3 feet from the side of the craft, the paddler seems to pull the paddle towards him, but it is, in fact, the canoe that moves. The paddler should withdraw the paddle once it is 6 inches from the side of the boat to avoid getting it stuck underneath it. He can either pull the blade from the water, or else turn it sideways and slip it back out ready to pull again.

If the bowman and stern-man both use complementary draw strokes, the canoe will pivot, turning quickly.

a)

b)

45 Draw stroke a) The paddle is placed in the water and the canoe will swivel towards the paddles, turning the canoe on the spot b) The draw stroke can be used to move the boat sideways without swivelling, by both paddles being used on the same side.

water in as big a semi-circle as he can manage, withdrawing the paddle near the stern. Used to turn a canoe, the top arm is kept bent while the pulling arm acts at full stretch. The more lean there is, the more effective the turn. The grip on the paddle can be altered to increase leverage, and the paddle is kept horizontal just above the gunwale. In a C2, the two paddlers use the opposite but complementary strokes for turning — the bowman using the bow stroke while the stern-man uses the stern stroke to effect a sharp turn.

Stern or reverse sweep The paddler does not lift the paddle clean out of the water as cleanly on the stern sweep. He pushes the blade forward but keeps both his arms bent for both the pushing and pulling actions. At the start of the stroke the blade is angled slightly to add a steering action before pulling through in a curve. The circle traced is usually smaller and the upper arm is kept lower.

Pivot turn This is an extension of the sweep stroke where the paddle jumps the bow and continues the sweep on the far side, tracing 180° through the water.

Draw stroke Kayakers stole this effective stroke from the canoeists. It is used to draw or move the canoe sideways. Placing the paddle in the water

36

Push-over stroke This is the opposite of the draw, and moves the canoe sideways away from the paddle as the paddler pushes on the blade.

J stroke The most famous Canadian canoe stroke, the J stroke is used to handle the unbalanced momentum that paddling on one side produces. Designed to keep the canoe going straight, a solo paddler uses it all the time because he cannot keep changing sides. The J refers to the shape of the stroke (on the left-hand side of the boat!) as the blade starts wide of the canoe at the bow and curves back in towards the paddler before curving away out again at the end.

There are several other subtleties which include getting the blade 'under' the gunwale, with the paddler's top hand out over the water, as well as turning the blade in the latter part of the stroke. The inside edge is eased from 90° to the boat round to 45° so that the stern of the canoe moves away from the paddling side in order to compensate for the one-sided impetus. The paddle actually scrapes along the gunwale towards the end of the stroke to take the pressure off the muscles of the lower arm. At the conclusion of the stroke, the paddle is again feathered as it is swung forward. Kept at an angle of 30°, thin and flat so that it won't be affected by hitting waves, the paddle is kept low, close to the water.

The J stroke is easier for the stern-man, since he has more room for his paddle at the end of the stroke as the canoe narrows towards the stern.

Cross draw There used to be a school of thought that frowned on paddlers changing sides. This thankfully has had its day, as canoeing is a practical sport. The cross draw is an example of crossing over from one side to another in order to turn the bow in slow moving water. Without changing grip drastically, the paddler slips his bottom hand up the shaft a little and executes a series of draw strokes. The paddle is not vertical but rather angled with the top hand below shoulder height as the paddler draws the bow round.

Pry Another turning stroke favoured by stern-men, where the paddle curves in towards the paddler before pushing or prying away at the water in a sort of reverse draw stroke.

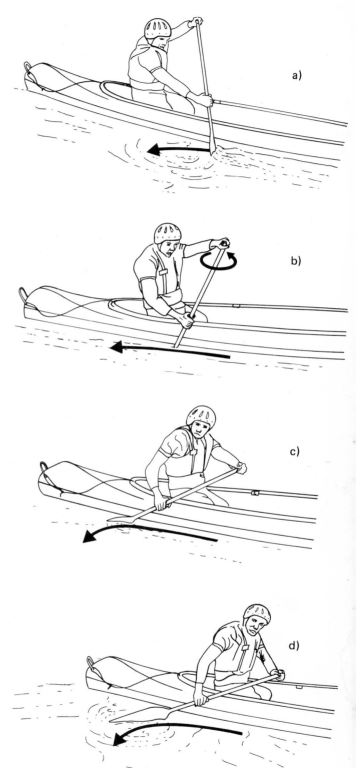

a)

b)

c)

d)

46 J stroke a) Start of stroke b) Starting to twist blade and push out c) Twisting blade and pushing out to cancel yawing of canoe d) Finish of stroke.

CHAPTER 4
Getting Started, the First Outing, and Care and Maintenance

First steps

The best way to get started in the sport is to join a local club. The reasons for this might not be obvious at first, but for the beginner there are many benefits. It can be an inexpensive way to find out whether it is kayaking or canoeing the beginner wants to pursue. A club is also a good source of reliable second-hand boats and, most important, a learner can find experienced teachers who will set him off on the right path. Annual subscriptions are usually reasonable, as are the coaching courses that teach the practical aspects of safety either in a swimming pool or on a quiet stretch of water. A recognized club would be the only organization allowed to use most swimming pools for practising rolling because a pool manager would not be too happy to see just any individual trying to drop a canoe or kayak into his pool, and far less happy seeing sharp-pointed, unprotected craft hitting the tiled sides! And, of course, a beginner needs advice in all the smaller details that go to make up a paddler's equipment — paddles, spray cover, anoraks, buoyancy aids, canoe helmets, etc.

Different conditions demand different equipment. If the club is based beside a canal or lake, then all that is needed at first is a buoyancy aid and a spray cover for comfort to stop the drips wetting the legs. An anorak comes later, as does a crash helmet which might be needed if the beginner is going to paddle on a shallow river where there is a chance of knocking his head.

It is always wise to ask a lot of questions at the club. Find out when they are running the sort of instructional courses that are needed, and what sort of canoeing is done. Some clubs specialize in competition, others will do competition as well as touring. However, by their very nature, canoeists are individual and like to do their own thing. So, once they have the ability, fans of touring like to go off on their own, away from the masses. By contrast, those who like competitions prefer to get together to improve their skills and to set up good training facilities. But whichever category of canoeing or kayaking the club specializes in, members will be able to advise on other aspects of the sport.

A club is always a good place to buy a second-hand — and therefore reasonably priced — boat. Talk to people about the boats on offer, try two or three out before making a commitment. Use common sense. Luckily, canoes are fairly easy to assess, unlike second-hand cars! Look over the canoe according to its type. If it is a canvas boat (and there are still a few around), then look for tears in the canvas. A beginner is not recommended, however, to buy a canvas boat because it is heavy and fragile and may well have been sitting on the side for a long time. Plywood canoes can be a good buy as they need little maintenance. It is easy to see if the varnish has rubbed off where it has been scraped or banged. Like anything made of wood, rot can be recognized by a stain or different colour where water is soaking into the boat. Some plywood boats are sewn together with nylon string which is then covered in fibreglass tape. If this has rubbed off, the string may need re-coating. If the seams are coming apart, be wary; the boat may have had a particularly hard life and there may be problems at each end of the craft that are not visible.

A fibreglass canoe is usually pigmented, with the colour built into it. If this is the case, look for fractures on the outside which are easy to spot. Press hard on a fracture to see how much it gives; if it stays fairly firm then there's a good chance that it is easy to repair. If the boat is clear, completely translucent, as many competition boats are, then the fracture will show up as a white mark. Surface scratches disappear when the boat is wet, so *never* look at a fibreglass boat when it is wet; wait until it has dried out.

It is very difficult to assess the inside of a kayak or canoe. Just look for the same faults as on the outside — cracks or bad marks. In a kayak, because there is only a small cockpit, it is difficult to assess the damage down at the end of the boat and often the blocks of foam used for buoyancy make it impossible to see right down to the end of the boat. But looking at the outside should give a good idea of the overall condition. The one thing that should be checked is the condition of the seam, where the hull and deck join. If the fibreglass is split on the inside it would need some repairs. Also check to see that the seat is fixed firmly and that there are no fibreglass edges under it or under the cockpit rim. Structural repairs are fairly simple to make on a fibreglass canoe but it is much harder to make cosmetic repairs.

Second-hand boats are not necessarily bad boats. People change competition boats for a variety of reasons: some sell when they decide not to compete any more; others can afford to buy a new model every season. These often are good value but since designs in the competition world change quickly, sound advice is very important.

Not that the beginner would be going for a competition model right away. Look for a good, all-round canoe or kayak to start with, one that will be versatile, while getting used to the different strokes. Once these are under control, the beginner can look around again and make a more definite choice about which model will suit him or her best for the next stage.

There is often a lot of mystique about paddles and this is unnecessary. Initially, paddles are usually flat, with both paddle blades at the same angle. This makes very little difference to start with compared with a 'feathered' paddle. But as soon as a beginner gets used to controlling the boat, the upper blade will be travelling through the air at 25 to 30 m.p.h. and this will cause a lot of wind resistance. To try to eliminate this, the blade is 'feathered' at 90°, which means that a right-handed paddle, known as 'right-handed control', is held firmly in the right hand and the shaft is slipped through the left. In this way, the right wrist — for most people the strongest — is doing the hard work. For the left-hander, it works the other way round. 'Feathering' makes paddling easier.

Beginners have to make sure they pick up the correct paddle as they are more likely to have problems if they have an unsuitable paddle.

The length of the paddle is governed by what aspect of the sport is being taken up, because competition and touring have different requirements. The cheapest paddles are aluminium with plywood blades. These give reasonable life, are reasonably light, with reasonable feel. They are very cold on the hands in cool weather, but not hot in summer.

The next paddle up the scale uses the same alloy shaft but with plastic blades at each end which have a slightly improved life. They tend to be a little bit heavier but are worth considering. Next there are wooden blades which are still thought to be the best because they are warmer, have a smoother feel and a more continuous spring. For the beginner who tends to do a lot of canoeing and can afford them, they are well worth the extra money.

As for the length of the paddle, that is governed by the boat as well as the paddler's physical stature. Graham Mackereth, the Olympic canoeist, recommends this easy test — 'Put the paddle facing you, keeping your shoulders straight, and stretch your hand up. You should be able to grip the top of the paddle by wrapping your fingers over the blade.' A generalization, of course, but a useful and quick guide.

It is worth noting that beginners usually take up the sport in single canoes or kayaks and there is no specific advantage in learning in a double craft. While an instructor could correct some faults more easily using a double, there is a danger that the beginner will take longer to get a 'feel' for the boat or to realize which hand is the stronger since the experienced paddler will always be making the correction. A single-seater is the best way for the beginner 'to get on with it'.

Picking up the canoe

A canoe is usually picked up by two people, one at each end. In North America, paddlers often 'portage' (as carrying is called) with just one person using the bar across the centre of the boat as a carrying yoke. The boat is lifted up, turned upside down and is carried across the shoulders. In this way, it can be carried easily from the top of a car down to the water, or from water to water if the portage is used to avoid a weir or other obstacle.

All canoes are designed to be used in water! They are not designed to be sat in or played in on dry land. Many can withstand this treatment but others will not, particularly if children bounce around on the seats. Canoes are designed to be as light as possible, so they give the paddler a good peformance. The design, therefore, anticipates the stress of people sitting on the seats to be transmitted throughout the whole boat *only* when it is on water.

On the water — the open canoe

The open canoe does not generally have a rope or

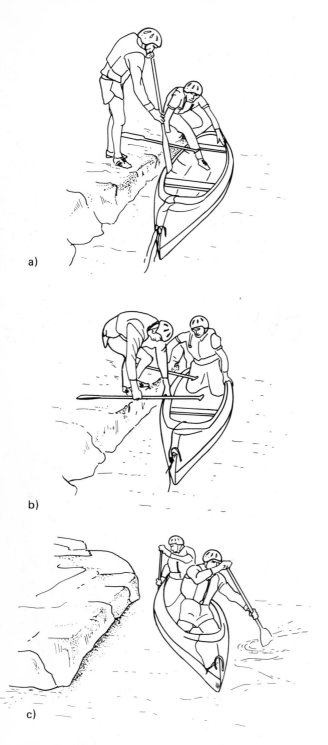

a)

b)

c)

47 Embarkation from the bank a) Sternman getting into the canoe b) Sternman kneeling and holding bank while bowman enters c) Draw stroking away *without* pushing off with paddles.

'painter' for tying up. Lines can be attached fore and aft if it is next to a landing stage but in shallow water one end is simply dragged up on to the bank, with the other end left floating. If the water is tidal, it is vital to check that the tide is not coming in . . . or the canoe will float away!

To get going in a family canoe, one person climbs in and walks gently to the far end of the boat, stepping on the strongest sections of the hull which are usually in the centre where there is most stability. Both hands should be on the side rails, or gunwales, and the bodyweight kept low while crossing over the seats. The canoeist should sit down on the seat at the end of the boat, pick up a paddle and dip the blade into the water so that it acts like an outrigger and stabilizes the boat. If the boat lurches at all, the paddler is immediately ready to pull or push at the water. The paddler's companion should pick up the bow of the boat, push it gently into the water and then, being an open canoe, just jump in. Open canoes are usually very stable.

If the canoe is in deep water, lying next to a bank or jetty, one paddler holds the boat as the other climbs aboard, picks up the paddle and places it gently on the bank, leaning as a balance while the second person gets in. Both paddlers can then push off from the side using their hands, rather than the paddles, which could be damaged pushing against a hard bank.

Picking up a kayak

A kayak is much lighter than a canoe — from 30 to 35 pounds, compared with double that for the more solid canoe. Therefore one person can easily pick up a kayak by the edge of the combing and walk along with it hanging by his side. Kayaks may also be carried on the shoulder.

On the water — the kayak

At the water's edge, whether it is deep or shallow, the kayak is usually placed parallel to the shoreline. Even if the water is shallow there is no need for the paddler to get wet feet, as the craft can be put in just a couple of inches of water. Once the paddler gets in, it is just a matter of doing up the spray cover and pushing away from the shore by hand, stretching down and pushing at the river bed. As in canoeing, it is better to use the hand rather than risk damaging the paddle, which should be resting across the boat ready for use.

There are at least two techniques for getting into a kayak when it is sitting in deep water. The 'approved' method is rather cumbersome. The paddle is placed

48 Individual world slalom champion Albert Kerr shows how one man carries a kayak.

a)

a) The paddler sits on back deck with his feet central holding firmly on to the bank and still keeping some weight on it b) The paddler slides into the cockpit and while still keeping hold of the bank and making sure his paddle is close by, straightens his legs and settles into the kayak.

b)

across the back of the cockpit with one blade on the bank and the other on the back deck. Holding the paddle, and adopting a crouching position, the paddler puts one leg at a time into the cockpit, always keeping the weight evenly distributed on the paddle. Then, sliding down into the boat, he puts the paddle in front of him across the boat and fits on the spray cover before paddling off.

Graham Mackereth prefers another way.

Because paddles vary so much in construction, a fibreglass shaft would be damaged by the 'approved' method and a wooden blade might be dented or scratched. Plastic-bladed, alloy-shafted paddles would be all right, especially as they are often used by beginners. However, I prefer to put the paddle across the *front* of the kayak, just resting there, but easy to get at when you need it. Then put one hand on the bank, the other on the centre of the cockpit, put your outside foot into the centre of the boat, well forward in the cockpit, keeping the weight equally distributed between both hands. Then bring the other foot across keeping your weight as low as you can. Slide your body in and pick up the paddle. If you can manage this way it is better as you are leaning forward and can see where you are going. What's more, you are less likely to damage your equipment.

50 Protection in a kayak a) Short cagoul over the tube of spray cover to give watertight seal.

b) The addition of buoyancy aid and mittens.

The only time the first method is really useful is if the water level is so high that the kayak is actually higher than the river bank.

Clothing

The weather conditions on a particular day dictate what clothing should be worn but a complete spare set of clothes should always be taken along, even on the first time out. These should be stored in a waterproof bag so they are dry if needed after a ducking. The overall guide to clothing is this — it should be inexpensive and warm and neither hold water nor restrict movement.

Once paddlers are in action, they get warm very quickly. In an open canoe, protection is needed all over; in a kayak, trousers are needed in the cold, but with a spray cover on everything underneath, inside the boat, will be warm in a few seconds. The upper body, however, would be cold without the right protection and a single-skin nylon anorak is particularly important to keep the spray off and the warmth in. If there is warm sunshine, its heat is intensified out on the water so it is wise to wear a hat and shirt to avoid sunburn, otherwise, jeans and a T shirt are adequate and, if it is chilly, add a sweater and anorak. A *quilted* anorak should never be worn, nor a hooded jacket. No one should ever go canoeing in anything that holds a lot of water and, for this reason, lightweight materials are best.

For the feet, ordinary sneakers, gym shoes or sand shoes are quite adequate and are certainly preferable to not wearing shoes at all. Riverbeds are scattered with sharp stones, glass and shells which can cut the feet badly and portages are hard on bare feet. However, boots or rubber shoes are strictly forbidden because these would quickly fill with water in the case of an accident and waterlogged boots are very heavy and cumbersome.

Hands are generally left bare because wearing gloves gives less 'feel' for the paddle and there is actually more chance of having an accident by dropping the paddle and then scrambling to get it. There are special canoeing mittens which cover the back of the hand, leaving the palm bare to hold the paddle. These are used on expeditions or if a chilly wind is blowing but they are not recommended for beginners. If it is cold enough for mittens, beginners should be wary about being out on the water.

The first outing

Once the beginner has sufficient strokes, he should go on a short expedition of a few hours on some gently flowing water. He should be competent enough not to ram everybody and everything in sight!

Rules of the road

'Power always gives way to sail,' and as a canoe is powered (by the paddler) it must always give way to sail. When it comes down to rowing boats versus canoes — 'if they look bigger than you, get out of the way, particularly if they are not looking where they are going,' is a common piece of canoeing lore. Always paddle down the right-hand side of the stream so that oncoming traffic is passed left-hand side to left-hand side ('port to port'). This is the opposite way to the British driving system but the same as nearly everyone else's.

Beware of fishing lines and don't antagonize fishermen!

It is worth remembering that many stretches of water are licensed, so canoeists and kayakists have to take out a ticket or licence, even on rivers that are public right of way. The money is used for maintaining the water. Many countries have special river guides which help with the planning of even the shortest, easiest expedition. It is worthwhile using them, as there is no point in setting off unprepared.

Example of river guide: Kangaroo River

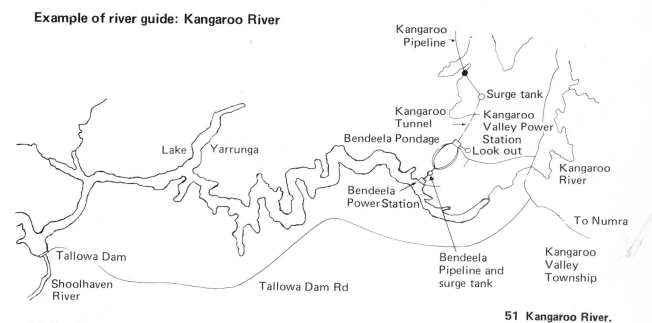

51 Kangaroo River.

LOCATION

Southern Tablelands. Flows generally south, south-west. The Upper Kangaroo commences below the Carrington Falls, and eventually flows into the Shoalhaven.

DESCRIPTION OF RIVER

Narrow and tree-lined. The reaches below Carrington Falls are little more than a creek with dense, rain forest vegetation. Canoeable sections commence from the suspension bridge in Upper Kangaroo Valley and continue to the junction of the Kangaroo and Shoalhaven Rivers. However, the Tallowa Dam, which is situated at this junction, causes the water to back-up to approximately 4 miles below Hampden Bridge in normal flow.

DISTANCE

Total between Suspension Bridge and Tallowa Dam:	— 25 miles
Sections: Suspension Bridge to Kelly's Road Bridge:	— 3 miles
Suspension Bridge to Hampden Bridge:	— 7 miles
Kelly's Road Bridge to Hampden Bridge:	— 4 miles
Hampden Bridge to Bendeela Pumping Station:	— 7 miles
Hampden Bridge to Urunga Creek:	— 15 miles
Hampden Bridge to Tallowa Dam:	— 18 miles

RIVER GRADES

Grades 1 and 2 mainly, with a couple of small Grade 3. Rapids are not large in volume of water, but because of the tree-lined nature of the river, at normal flow they can be very tricky with varying degrees of difficulty.

ACCESSIBILITY

Good for sections above Hampden Bridge. Below the bridge, access is either the Pumping Station (right-hand bank going downstream) or Urunga Creek (also right-hand bank 3 miles above the junction) or Tallowa Dam itself (left-hand bank). Care must be taken to pull in upstream of red warning buoys which are stationed 400 metres upstream of the dam wall. If continuing downstream on the Shoalhaven, portage around the dam on the left-hand bank — there is a rough trail supplied by the dam authorities.

RIVER HEIGHT

CAMP SITES

Good camping generally.

HAZARDS

In the section between the Suspension Bridge and Kelly's Road Bridge there are two tree hazards which should be approached with caution. The first can be waded around via a flood channel on the right, and the second is immediately below where the flood channel joins the main stream again. The second hazard being a large fallen tree right across the river and should be regarded as a danger spot. Recommendations for the second hazard: If sufficiently skilled (be honest in your self-appraisal) canoeists can either:

1) Cross the mainstream and break into an eddy on left bank immediately above the tree and portage around the root section.

2) Enter mainstream and break into eddy on right bank *immediately* upstream of log, get out and carefully lift canoes over the log, taking care that the canoe is not caught by force of water in a 'cockpit facing upstream' situation.

3) Beginners or novice paddlers should rope or line down to log and portage around it.

A further hazard also encountered in this section is a washed-out bridge (twisted metal bridgework and fallen concrete blocks, caused by flood damage).

On a short trip with beginners it is good to aim for a pre-determined site. There a helpful friend or parent can wait with a picnic so that the young paddler can eat and rest before the return journey. A day's outing will soon develop into a weekend or a week-long holiday, commonly called 'touring'. Just as Boy Scouts, cyclists or hikers go camping, so too do paddlers. After all, the sport is all about enjoying natural beauty, and camping out is part of the fun.

In some countries there are small inns or youth hostels available but canoeing and camping have traditionally gone hand in hand. All the rules governing camping apply to canoe touring. There is a temptation to take too much equipment since so much can be stored away, but if any portaging is to be done, a lighter boat makes a real difference!

A variety of comfortable dry clothing is always a boon, and a first aid kit is handy. Torches, spare blankets, stoves — all the items needed on a normal camping trip should be taken and shared amongst the group.

Once on the river the leader should stay up front with another experienced paddler shepherding the group along. The boats should keep a reasonable distance apart, and two canoes should never be on any rapids together.

Planning a trip

Before planning a long trip, especially one that goes into wilderness areas, a checklist should be drawn up to make sure that nothing is ignored or forgotten. Simple headings will remind organizers of the details that must be checked.

Objective

What is the destination, what is the route and how long will the journey take?

52 Recreational canoeing and kayaking is the most popular aspect of the sport worldwide. Here two paddlers are relaxing on Lake Toro in Canada (*G. Mackereth*).

The group

Are all the members experienced enough to undertake the journey, are they fit and healthy enough? Is the group well balanced: are there enough boys/girls, young, old?

Leaders

There should be one leader for about five group members. Have these been designated? Have they each got an assistant group leader to help them? Are they experienced and confident in their ability? Do they understand their duties? Are the leaders compatible? Is there someone competent to do first aid, rescue techniques and lifesaving?

The route

Do all members know about the proposed route? Has *all* available information about the route been obtained? Are there any unusual hazards, difficult portages? Have all permissions been sought? And what about water conditions, weather conditions? Are there suitable camp sites planned, emergency communications organized? *Remember* – a complete and detailed copy of the itinerary should be left with a responsible authority.

Administration

Is there a record of all the participants, along with their home addresses and telephone numbers? Does anyone suffer from any allergies or other medical conditions that might need special treatment? Is there a record of all the food and equipment that has been taken? It can be useful to plan menus ahead of time. Is *everyone (and every boat) properly insured?* If vehicles are involved for transport or to meet up along the route – are they and their trailers etc. in good working condition? Do their drivers have full details of the itinerary as well as emergency instructions?

Canoes

Are they in good condition? Are they the right craft for the trip? Have they been filled too full with either paddlers or equipment? Are they balanced? Is there spare equipment such as extra paddles? Are there flares and repair kits?

En route

Is there a log-book? Is it being kept? It is worth recording any difficulties encountered.

After the trip

It is invaluable to assess the experience both for the members of the trip and members of future expeditions. A final report is well worth the effort.

Care and maintenance

Any maintenance work should be undertaken only

when the craft is dry and free of grease. All patches and glueing should be done when the surfaces are well 'keyed', roughened to give grip.

Wood canoes

Any wooden canoe or canoe with a wooden frame will need a thorough overhaul at least once a year. This usually involves rubbing it down and giving it a revarnish. Wood should always have a minimum of three good layers of varnish on it but four or five will make the craft more durable. The paddler has to judge how much varnish is left on after a hard season and old varnish should always be 'cut back' with a medium sandpaper and then lightly sanded with a medium grade sandpaper, then can be used 'wet' or 'dry', such as a '240 wet and dry'.

If there are any bad gouges or cracks in the wood these should be repaired with wood filler. Any damage to an all-wood boat with a carved or smooth outside will need 'piecing' which should be undertaken by a skilled carpenter. If it is a 'stitch and glue' type wooden craft then a small fibreglass patch can be used if the owner does not feel like attempting to insert another piece of plywood. If an insertion is to be made, the plywood should be carefully cut to the shape of the hole, and then a butting piece should be put on the inside with at least a 1-inch overlap. When glued and screwed into the original boat and varnished over, it should provide a good watertight seal.

Wooden frames may need replacing if broken. However, a solid, open canoe with wood frames can be repaired by adding a rib rather than replacing it, butting up another wood frame against the side. If the ribs are made of oak then they can be steam-bent by using a steam oven but this is usually beyond the ability of a normal home builder who would do better to contact a boatyard or a skilled carpenter.

A broken stringer can be cut out of the boat and replaced, or a piece can be scarf-jointed across the back of it as a temporary repair, glued and bound on with twine.

Any screws loose that cannot be tightened up should be replaced with a screw one size larger. If, however, the wood is becoming rotten then it should be cut out and replaced. If a quick repair is needed, the rotten wood can be gouged out as far as the good timber and then filled in with an epoxy glue or a wood filler so that a screw will hold. This is not as satisfactory as a proper wood replacement but will do for a mid-season repair until the job can be done properly.

Wooden canoes should never be left out of doors when not in use. Occasionally for short periods during summer it does them no harm, but if kept indoors they will last longer, although they may tend to dry out. The best state therefore is a covered natural atmosphere. If boats are put into too dry and warm an atmosphere this can cause more problems than leaving them outside because the planks contract and gaps open up. When put back in the water they will leak for a short period until the water is absorbed back into the wood, and then they should become watertight again. This will not occur with the stitch and glue system or with plywood boats but only with very old wooden boats, built from traditional methods. When stored outdoors, canoes and kayaks should be kept on blocks 1 foot to 18 inches above the ground. This will allow the air to get inside them and ventilation is important because if the damp remains the wood will soon rot. As long as it has reasonable ventilation the boat should continue to give good service, though the danger areas are the ends, which are difficult to ventilate. When ripped, canvas is repaired by sewing the dges of the tear together with sailmaker's thread and a needle and then putting a patch over this, giving at least 1 inch to 1½ overlap all the way round. Nowadays the special proofing solutions that should be applied to the patch are available from tent repairers and manufacturers as the canoe building trade rarely builds in wood and canvas.

Reinforced plastic and fibreglass canoes

Most of today's canoes are made of reinforced plastic which can be left outside without any harm. These are very strong and durable boats, and if any damage occurs then the easiest and quickest way to do a temporary repair is to get some cloth-backed carpet tape and stick it over the crack or hole. This will do to keep the boat afloat for a weekend or two. But when a proper repair is made the surface must be bone-dry.

The most common repair necessary to a fibreglass boat is for a 'gel coat crack'. The gel coat sometimes cracks under stress when a boat knocks against a rock, or contracts in a pressure wave underneath a rapid. It looks like a very thin hairline fracture of the surface of the boat, usually in the hull. If this is only a minor crack it is not worth bothering about but if it requires repair the canoeist gouges out the damaged area with a chisel. Care must be taken not to gouge too deep, because the next layer of fibreglass material probably has not been badly damaged. Then a small amount of resin is mixed with colouring material to match the hull, the damaged area is filled in and some Melanex sheet is put over the top to give it a nice smooth finish. When the resin has cured (dried off) the Melanex sheet is peeled off and any surplus is eased off with a chisel. Most white water craft have clear hulls to make repairs easier, with no colour matching required.

If there is a more serious hole or crack then all the cracked fibreglass should be chiselled out and the repair should be done from the inside. The edge of this crack or hole should be heavily scoured and etched to get rid of any dirt or grease and to rough up the surface in order to give the best possible key for the repair materials. A piece of Melanex sheet should cover the hole or crack and then, working from the inside, it should be painted with layers of material and glass matt, as in the original lay up of the craft. As this is usually one layer of glass matt followed by fibreglass cloth, polyester cotton or kevlar cloth, the layers of material should be cut to the shape of the crack and, if deep into the bow or stern, inserted with the end of a stick and pushed into the right position with another stick. A 1-inch brush attached at right angles to the end of another stick can paint in the resin as well as push the material into the crack. One last layer of fibreglass matt should cover over the crack leaving at least 1 inch all the way round the crack or hole.

Again, the Melanex is peeled off, any surplus is eased off with a chisel, and the craft should be ready for the water.

If a wooden strengthener or glassfibre strengthener in an RP craft has broken, this too can be repaired. Strengtheners provide more of a frame for the outer layer of glass which has the maximum strength. Therefore it is not necessary to replace a wooden strengthener. Clean out the crack, paint resin into it and then put two layers of matt plus a finishing layer of the same material as the original strengthener over the top. This should ensure that the strength is replaced.

All repairs should be done on the inside and it is useful to ask the manufacturer for some spare samples of the material from which the boat has been built. These can be used to get a finish which looks like the original finish of the boat. If all repairs are done on the inside, the results will be neat and tidy. This helps to maintain the second-hand value of the boat, too, in spite of the repairs.

It is possible to make a repair in a white water boat too strong. The problem is that the hull of a white water boat is depressed as it bounces against

rocks on a downstream run. If the boat has an even rigidity, it just slides off the rocks. But if a rock happens to strike an overstrong patch, the hull will begin to crack around it and the patch will soon fall off.

It is important to use first quality resin and better to use an isopthallic polyester or a vinyl ester resin (which have better mechanical bonding power than standard resins used in general lay-ups). This means that the patch is less likely to peel off the boat. So the extra money and extra time required for this repair will be repaid as the value of the boat stays higher and the life of the patch is longer.

One of the most common problems of a modern slalom boat is that the ends get broken off. They are so thin and the stresses on them from the paddlers and the rocks are so great that something sooner or later has to give, usually the end of the boat. If the craft is made of a material such as kevlar, then the ends are unlikely to be broken; they will just fold. This is because kevlar is very strong but the resin that reinforces it is weaker and can shatter under too great a stress. The canoeist has to straighten out the end of the boat, scrape off all the flaky resin and apply a new layer which will soak into the kevlar.

Polyester fabric (more commonly known as diolen) reacts in a similar way. Glassfibre will, however, just snap in half, and the way to mend it is to use something to hold it together — a wire coat hanger around the end of the boat can be a cheap solution. Canoe dealers would tend to use a wooden batten fixed to the side, top or bottom of the boat in order to make it retain its original position. The professionals try to reinforce the nose from the inside. More layers are needed to give extra strength because the rigidity is all-important at the ends, in contrast to further down the boat where extra layers of glass are more likely to 'crack out' on impact. At the ends, the deck is so rigid that two extra layers of reinforcing will do more good than harm.

The buoyancy foam often needs to be taken out when doing an internal repair. There are two types used inside most boats now. Polystyrene, the old type, can be pulled out once the piece of glassfibre that hold it in place is cut. The replacement piece can only be stuck into the hull and deck with vinyl ester resin; polyester resin will dissolve the polystyrene unless masked by masking tape. Nowadays polyether foam is more common as it will stick to the hull and deck with polyester resin. To remove it, the canoeist has to use a very sharp knife blade (something like a hacksaw blade with an edge ground on to it) to cut away the foam block by running the blade up each side of the hull and deck. It is more difficult to remove polyether foam but it does provide greater strength for the boat and does not fall out as easily as polystyrene.

Aluminium canoes

If aluminium canoes need patching, the patch has to be affixed to the outside with epoxy resin. Sometimes known as a 'tingle' (which can be used on a wooden boat as well), the patch would also be riveted to ensure that it will not fall off. ABS boats and rotationally moulded polyethylene should not need repairing. The odd bolt or foot rest may need replacing but that should be the extent of the problems. These boats are more expensive initially but care and maintenance are very much less. All plastic boats should, however, be kept out of strong sunlight. The same goes for wood which will fade slowly in colour over the years. ABS and polyethylene boats tend to become brittle if left in strong sunlight. While the early ABS and polyethylene materials were not, or had very limited, ultra-violet protection, the new materials are, but will very slowly degrade over many years so they should be kept out of strong sunlight where possible.

Paddles

The care and maintenance of paddles is often ignored. Wooden paddles should always be retouched when the varnish gets scratched, in order to stop water getting in, staining the paddle and leading to rot. This will drastically shorten the life of the paddle compared to a reinforced plastic one. If an RP blade fractures, some resin can be run into it and a small patch put on to help hold it together. There is no repair for an alloy shaft. Once dented it will soon break and once the oval or circular shape is warped the paddle is as good as broken, since it will eventually fold at that point; however, new shafts are not expensive.

There is no long-term maintenance for RP blades. They should withstand an awful lot of wear and tear but any cracks must be filled. If they are foam-filled blades and the end starts wearing through, then the foam must not get wet because it soaks up water, becomes far heavier and is almost impossible to dry out. Some foam-filled blades expand in very hot climate, so they should be kept out of the heat. The same goes for ABS blades. They degrade slowly in strong sunlight.

A good suggestion is to put a small ring of tape across the paddle shafts to mark the paddling position and to stop the hands from slipping down out of position.

Other equipment

Any other equipment and clothing should always be dried out after canoeing. If the paddler has been in dirty water, particularly water polluted by chemical effluent, then the paddler should not only wash down properly but also clean the boat, paddles and especially his anorak and spray cover. Chemicals often disturb the waterproofing of clothing which can be neoprene-proofed and polyurethane-proofed. If an anorak is torn it can easily be stitched back together, adding a patch on the outside for extra strength. If an anorak seam goes, try to stitch it the way the manufacturer originally did. Good anoraks have waterproofed seams. Once this seal has been broken an easy way to reproof the seams is to use a thick contact adhesive which will remain fairly flexible and waterproof until it peels off. Then it is fairly easy to apply a little more to the area.

Helmets need no maintenance as they are generally made of nylon or polycarbonate. If the outer shell breaks there is little that can be done, although if part of the helmet breaks away from one of the rivets it is possible to obtain a new one. Fortunately, helmets are not very expensive and if there are any problems it is best to be safe and buy a new one.

Buoyancy aids must always work satisfactorily. If they have a zip on the front and the zip sticks it should be replaced. There is no point in a paddler having a buoyancy aid that pops open when he is swimming. It is also better to have a buoyancy aid with a tie on it as well as a zip, as an added safeguard.

Wetsuits should never be kept folded up in a drawer. At the end of the season they should be talcum-powdered and put away on a broad, soft-shouldered hanger that can take the weight.

Points of safety

DOs and DON'Ts

Swimming You must be able to swim 50 yards unaided in the clothing in which you go canoeing, before you even think of going out in a canoe.

Buoyancy You must wear a buoyancy aid whenever you are on the water.

Stay together Do go canoeing in a group if at all possible and do keep together.

Stay close Do stay near to shore so that if you capsize it is an easy swim back.

Watch the weather Avoid going canoeing if it is cold and windy until you are experienced enough to deal with any accident that might occur.

Equipment Always check that your equipment is serviceable *before* setting out.

Clothing Do take a spare set of clothing in a waterproof kit bag, just in case you capsize.

Overload Do not overload your canoe.

Swim for it If capsized, do not try to right the canoe. It will hold air and float upside down — so swim with it to the bank.

Steer clear Avoid powered craft, skiffs and sailing boats. They might not be able to see you as well as you can see them.

Off the hook Anglers pay to fish, so respect their wishes and pass by quietly on the far side of the river or canal. There is plenty of room for everyone.

Two's company Never go paddling alone on moving water.

Mind your head Always wear a crash helmet when paddling on moving water.

Beware of weirs Always avoid weirs, they are always dangerous.

Bank it Swim straight for the nearest bank if you capsize — never upstream.

Stay up Stay upstream of a capsized canoe. Keep your feet off the riverbed as there may be some sharp rocks or glass.

Push off Float on your back, pushing off rocks with you feet, keeping your feet downstream.

Check out Always tell someone where you are planning to paddle and when you expect to return.

Before anyone steps into a canoe or kayak, he or she must be prepared for an accidental capsize. The first and most important rule is that paddlers *must be able to swim at least fifty yards wearing light clothing.*

Personal safety

For personal safety a waistcoat-like buoyancy aid or lifejacket of an approved and tested design *must* be used so that there is enough buoyancy to hold the person up. By far the most popular style for canoeing is the waistcoat-type filled with solid foam, or a closed-cell foam which is usually covered in nylon to make it more attractive. For a lifejacket to be 'approved' it usually has to be able to turn an unconscious person's face upwards, above the surface of the water, as well as supporting him in the water.

All approved lifejackets have a certain amount of closed-cell foam inside but have to be inflated with air to be fully effective. Many experts are against them for this reason, because 'If you are unconscious, how are you going to be able to inflate it?' There is a big pouch on the chest with a tube that goes round the neck to support the head, rather like the lifejackets demonstrated by air hostesses on aeroplanes. One expensive version has a compressed air cylinder which activates as soon as the paddler hits the water so that the jacket automatically inflates. In the rest, a cord has to be pulled. There is another danger with this type — if punctured, the buoyancy just hisses away!

Whatever aid is used, it must be adjusted to suit the user's weight. Lifejackets have a system of straps at the back so that people of any size can wear them. Many beginners wonder if they need a helmet right from the start. Although they should never be in a situation where they could bang their heads, there is always a chance that an overhanging branch rather than an underwater rock will take the novice by surprise. For this reason it is worth investing in an inexpensive protection for the head. Helmets do not really come into their own until the paddler is on moving water with eddies and waves. When

53 A paddler in action properly equipped with crash helmet and buoyancy aid. Note the need for a spray cover! (*G. Mackereth*).

the water is playing tricks the paddler tends to lean the wrong way, which makes the boat turn over with the resulting danger of a bang on the head. Helmets are compulsory, of course, for slalom and white water competitors.

Boat safety

The second safety requirement concerns the boat. It should be made so that it is impossible to sink.

The canoe The problem with an open canoe is simply the fact that it is open. This means that it has not got the natural buoyancy of a kayak, so some canoes have airtight compartments fitted at each end. These are usually sufficient. If they are not fitted, then it is sensible to buy a large buoyancy bag which is available from most canoe stores. This is tied to the centre of the boat. Remember to see that it is tied securely or zipped up properly and that the seat is fixed firmly in place.

For beginners, the more air that can be trapped in the boat, the better. Then, if there is an accident and water does get in, it will be easier to rescue the canoe. There is also far less chance of damage as it is dragged up on to the bank or as people try to lift it out of the water.

Before putting the boat in the water make sure both it and the paddle are serviceable. Obviously, if there are any holes or suspect cracks in the boat,

they should be repaired at once. Good paddlers never take chances.

Sometimes the boat is damaged while away from base and to cover this eventuality, a roll of heavy-duty sticky tape (such as self-adhesive, sticky-backed carpet tape) is the canoeist's best friend. It is the easiest repair kit around and should be kept handy. However, in order for the tape to stick properly, the boat must be bone-dry before it is applied to any suspect cracks that might let in water.

Spray sheets/spray decks/spray covers These can be fitted to open canoes as well as kayaks, and can save many a spill. There are various types on the market, each suitable for different sorts of boats. The only time an open canoe is fitted with a spray cover would be in very rough conditions that no beginner would or should be near. For safety's sake, they should be tested before a trip starts so that the users are totally confident that they can release themselves quickly. Time should be spent practising releases, rather than struggling when an emergency occurs. This means that the loops on kayak spray covers should be firmly attached on the *inside*.

The kayak The requirements for a kayak are basically the same as for a canoe in terms of safety. However, the ends of the boat carry small loops with plastic or wooden toggles on them which make it easier to pick up the kayak. Kayaks are often fitted with a 'deckline' that runs from end to end, and this should go through some sort of clip or loop at the side of the cockpit so that it cannot narrow in, or ride up over the cockpit itself and get caught up round the paddler. Some people use a shorter line running from the bow to a point in front of the cockpit. More decorative than useful most of the time, these lines are a help when towing a boat during a rescue. In general, though, the more bits of rope and extra gadgets on a boat, the more likely a beginner is to get tangled up in them.

As for buoyancy, most kayaks have foam blocks tailored to fit between the hull and the deck. These prevent sinking and at the same time add strength to the deck which therefore does not need to be as heavy. This keeps the craft as light as possible. Nonetheless, it is still a good idea to add extra buoyancy bags for beginners.

Methods of survival

Capsizing (Canoe) Beginners *must* practise falling out, so that when they do capsize they do not panic. Falling out of a canoe is very simple, the paddler just leans further and further over to one side until he or she falls out. Canoes are very stable, very "beamy", so they are hard to overturn completely. If they tip over, the paddler usually falls out but the canoe bobs back upright! There is very little in a canoe that can trap the paddler though he should automatically hold on to his paddle. Any other equipment in the boat should have been tied down firmly to the seats or thwarts so it does not fall out and float away.

Coming back up to the surface after capsizing and still holding on to the paddle, the canoeist gets hold of the end of the boat. If it is the right way up, he puts the paddle back into the canoe and simply swims to the bank pushing his boat ahead of him. If the canoe has turned over, he leaves it that way and swims with it back to the bank or to shallow water before righting it. Canoes are so light and buoyant that they are easy to manoeuvre.

Capsizing (kayak) The capsizing drill is more complicated and is often practised in a swimming pool or in clear, clean water at least 3 feet deep. Working in the warm water of a pool fills beginners with confidence and they don't mind capsizing a few times. Because the body slips into a kayak under a protective spray cover, there is a possibility of becoming trapped inside unless care is taken. The paddler should never cross his legs or jam himself in. One instructor says, 'When people panic they can do amazing contortionist acts; they have strength and power you can never believe they would have. I've seen a big chap pull his boat apart in his panic!'

As long as the paddler does not panic when turned upside down, capsizing out of a kayak is easy. It is sensible to practise calmly in a swimming pool and to start without a spray cover or a paddle. Holding the side of the boat, he should rock it, so he rolls over. Once the boat is upside down, he grabs hold of the cockpit, as illustrated in fig. 54 (a), pushes (b) and (c), does a forward somersault motion and so comes out of the boat, surfaces and holds on to his boat (d). The somersault movement brings the legs out so that they cannot become entangled or trapped.

Once on the surface the paddler leaves the boat upside down and swims with it to the side of the pool. Many beginners try to right their craft while swimming but this only brings more water sloshing into the kayak, making it harder to control. When a kayak overturns it floats easily because of the buoyancy aids and the air trapped inside.

There are two ways of emptying a kayak. If there is only a little water inside, it is very easy. Going into a shallow spot the paddler puts his head up under the boat in the cockpit and stands up. Using his

54 Capsizing out of a kayak.

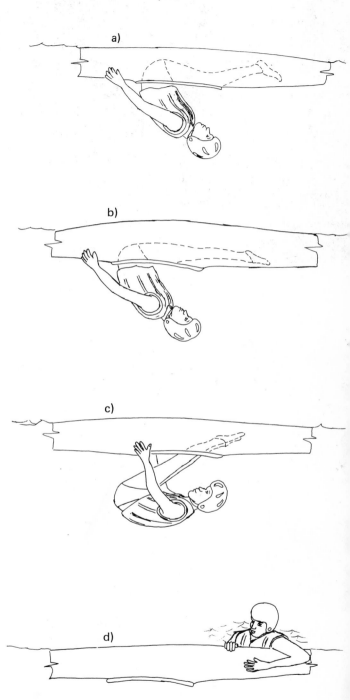

a)

b)

c)

d)

body as a pivot, he rocks the kayak backwards and forwards to let the water drain out. If there is a lot of water in the boat just pick up one end and let the water pour out. Keep using this see-saw action until enough water flows out so that the job can be finished by using the first method.

If for some reason there are no buoyancy bags in the kayak there may be so much water that two people are needed to empty it, again lifting each end alternately in a see-saw action.

Once the beginner is happy and confident about the escape drill (and the more practice the better!) the next step is a drill for capsizing with a spray cover on. Unlike escaping from a canoe, the paddler lets go of the paddle as soon as the kayak is turned upside down. This leaves both hands free to pull the toggle or strap which releases the spray cover. Then, after counting two, he executes the forward roll, comes out of the kayak and up to the surface.

Rolling Rolling is a technique which enables a paddler who has turned upside down to bob up on the other side. It is a quick movement to complete the 360° turn, surprising to watch and with a mystique all its own. No one knows for sure how old the idea of rolling actually is. It was developed by the Eskimos because of the extreme conditions of the Arctic. If they were out hunting and were charged by walrus or capsized in rough seas, they could not come out of the boat and try to swim to safety because they would have died of cold. The only way was to right the overturned boat while still inside it — and to do it quickly. Moreover, as these small boats were also used to carry passengers who would lie down inside, the roll meant not just the survival of the hunter but perhaps his family as well.

The Eskimos relied totally on driftwood to construct their boats and paddles and the latter tended to be thin. This helped them while hunting since the paddles were very quiet in the water, but the blades were small so that they had to use a special technique now called 'put across' in order to get the necessary leverage to right themselves. Nowadays the 'put across' is seldom used as it takes longer than other versions of the roll. The drawback was the extra time spent in cold water, but since it was deep there was no chance of head injury.

Modern rolls are faster, designed to get paddlers back in an upright position in white water. A shorter paddle with a broader blade helps because it has more 'power', that is, it gets more purchase on the water. The 'Pawlata roll' is the first one to master, then the 'screw roll' and some advanced paddlers

become so adept they can roll using just one hand. A useful skill if a paddle is lost!

Edi Hans Pawlata was an Austrian and the first European to perform the Eskimo roll. While studying sociological papers written about Eskimo life, he suddenly discovered they had developed a roll. He was already a kayaker and taught himself the technique which everyone else then copied.

To learn the 'Pawlata roll', the right-handed paddler starts with the paddle on his left-hand side, sitting upright. Before he actually capsizes he holds the end of the blade in his left hand, with his hand tucked underneath the blade. The blade is at 90° to the surface of the water, and his right-hand is about 2 feet 6 inches from his left-hand, down the shaft towards the other end of the blade, with his wrist cocked around the shaft.

He then capsize rolls to the left-hand side, going completely underwater. Upside down now he pushes the blade down, which means he is feeling for the surface of the water. When he has found the surface of the water, he pushes his right-hand out, tucking his left-hand behind him. He sweeps the blade across the surface of the water and pulls on it at the same time. He needs to angle the blade, as he does when he is sculling for support, and the effect of sweeping that across the surface of the water will pull him up. When he gets to effectively 90° to the central line of the boat he will find that he can't twist any further than that and then he's got to feather it the other way and bring it back on himself, and then he'll get the remainder of the power he needs to pull him up.

It is very helpful to have someone in the water alongside the learner who can guide the blade across the surface of the water, so that the learner gets the feel of it and gets the angle right.

It is best to learn in shallow water such as a swimming pool. In fact before attempting the stroke it is a good idea for the beginner to go to the side of the swimming pool, leaning with one hand on the bank, and letting the boat go upside down before pulling himself back up just using his hands. A lot of the secret of rolling is being able to flick the hips back up. To get the boat upright the paddler leaves his body in the water as long as possible because of the buoyancy that the body has. Everyone is tempted to get his head out of the water first, but in actual fact, to be able to roll successfully the head should be the *last* thing to come out of the water. Paddlers should try to keep their heads in the water till the last possible instant. Having practised this flick roll just with the hips, using the hands against

55 Competitor rolling out of trouble at the Llangollen town slalom (*Graham Ingram-Monk*).

the side of the pool, the next thing the paddler does is to capsize away from the side of the swimming pool. He should then reach for the side of the baths with his hands and pull himself up again. The idea is to get the confidence of going over one way carrying on through 360° to appear on the other side. The paddler can then go on from that to taking his paddles with him and capsizing in the shallow end — though not so shallow that he hits his head on the bottom, but shallow enough so that he can push himself off the bottom of the pool with his paddle. This will help him later on when he is practising rolling on his own. If he fails he can always push himself up without having to use his escape drill.

The main problem is that beginners get disoriented once they turn upside down in the water. Therefore the more that they are helped by other people to get the motion right initially, so they can 'feel' where they are in the water, the better. And even when paddlers succeed the first time it may not be the answer. They may find it still needs several more tries to recapture the secret.

Some paddlers find that the first time they try it, they roll quite successfully. Then they may not roll again successfully for ten days. The first one may come within the first few minutes of learning to roll, but it will take weeks before a paddler can do it automatically.

It has to end up being a very natural action, pivoting around the hips, using the boat as the pivot, with the head being the last thing coming through.

The screw roll is identical to the Pawlata, except that the hands are kept in a normal paddling condition. The advantage of this roll is that it is quicker to perform and in an emergency the paddler never has to take his hands off the paddle. He just leaves them there, as he does with the Pawlata, except that his right-hand is in the same place further down the

53

shaft and his left-hand is in its normal paddling position on the shaft. In the same way as the Pawlata he feels for the surface of the water, keeping the paddle angled, but instead of doing such a long stroke he probably does two or three short strokes. Once he becomes proficient and confident and he maximizes his hip action, he can come up on one stroke very easily.

Again he is using leverage against the water to pull himself back upright. One short, sharp stroke is all that's necessary. When the beginner is trying this, or the Pawlata roll, with someone giving a hand, very often all that's required is setting the correct angle of the paddle blade on the surface of the water. As the paddle is swept through the water one hand is kept underneath just to help to give it a little bit of pressure, so that he can pull on that. Very little pressure will often bring the paddler upright even though he may seem to be having some problems. Once he's got the angle right and he is pulling at a reasonable speed there is no reason why he shouldn't come upright.

Rafting up This is simply a way of joining canoes or kayaks together to form a raft. Stable and solid, rafting up may be used to give paddlers a rest or a chance to take photographs. It may also be used as a safety measure in rough conditions or to get all other boats out of the way if one craft is in trouble. If lost, paddlers are more likely to be spotted as a group than as individual craft.

Rafting should be done as soon as the pre-arranged signal is given. The leader will whistle or shout and raise his paddle (in calm conditions) or his arm (if it is windy). Boats form a line, one next to another, with the paddles providing a transverse support. Each paddler holds his paddle at one end so that the other end may be grasped by the next along. With each person holding on to two paddles the row should be steady and secure.

First aid

Hypothermia and the effects of cold
Before the term 'hypothermia' became generally known, people were said to have died of 'exposure', that is, being exposed to cold, wet weather. Since water sports enthusiasts can get wet at any time, they must avoid becoming cold and tired as well. This cold-wet condition has been called 'the number one killer of outdoor recreationists' by the US Forest Service; they describe it as 'the rapid, progressive mental and physical collapse accompanying the chilling of the inner core of the human body . . .

caused by exposure to cold, aggravated by wet, wind and exhaustion.'

Since hypothermia begins with the loss of surface heat it is important to keep the body well insulated. Clothing is the main protection and generally the more clothes worn the better, particularly if the outer layer is waterproof. Sensible as a shield against bad weather, proper clothing can save a life in case of capsizing in cold water, where the naked body loses heat 26 times more rapidly than in the air.

The sooner the individual is out of the water the better, but movement quickens heat loss and researchers at the University of Victoria in Canada have found that 'survival time in cold water is increased by about one-third simply by holding still instead of swimming.' They found that the average person is able to swim much less than one mile in water at 50°F before being incapacitated by cold, so their recommendation is *never* to swim to shore unless the distance really is less than a mile or the water is warm.

A lifejacket and knowledge of survival swimming techniques will extend the survival time in water.

This table gives an idea of how chilling and fatal even the warmest water can be.

Effect of immersion in water on the human body

Water Temp.	Exhaustion/ Unconsciousness	Survival
32°-40° F	15-30 mins	30-90 mins
40°-50° F	30-60 mins	1-3 hours
50°-60° F	1-2 hours	1-6 hours
60°-70° F	2-7 hours	2-40 hours

Signs and symptoms
1. Increasing slowness in physical and mental responses.
2. Irrational behaviour or irritability.
3. Difficulties with speech or vision.
4. Cold to the touch.
5. Slow, weak or imperceptible pulse.
6. Slow and shallow breathing.

Treatment
1. Remove the individual from the cold environment.
2. Protect from inclement conditions with some form of shelter.
3. Remove all wet clothing and place in a situation where the body can gradually recover its proper temperature, i.e. (a) sleeping bag, (b) between two people, etc.

Warming

Sudden extremes of warming will precipitate a surge of warm blood away from the deep tissues and so cause a fatal drop in the patient's blood pressure and temperature.

In all cases hospitalization is necessary as soon as possible and expert medical help should be sought. At all times standard first aid procedure must be carried out. Moving a patient suffering from hypothermia should be delayed, if shelter and protection are immediately available and if conditions admit, until some recovery has been achieved. Evacuation should then be undertaken by stretcher or an improvised litter. Any other form of carrying creates circulation problems which may induce a relapse.

Cramp

Cramp is an involuntary shortening of the muscle often caused during exercise by poor co-ordination, poor blood circulation, chilling (as in swimming) or an excessive loss of salt (as in extreme sweating).

Occurrence: Calf of leg   50%
                Hand or foot 25%
                Thigh   15%

Treatment It is normal to stretch the muscle against its contracting spasm and to massage it firmly.

Self-management

Calf: Straighten the knee and with your hands draw the foot up towards the shin: or, straighten the toes and stand on the ball of the foot.

Thigh: Straighten knee and push thigh forward.

Although cramp is common enough, it often causes the victim to panic and it is the panic that kills, not the cramp. If cramp strikes, paddlers should always remember to relax. They will have other limbs that function perfectly well . . . so they should use them!

Asphyxia

A constant supply of oxygen is required by the body for the normal functions of life to be carried out efficiently. This oxygen supply is carried in the air. When the lungs do not get a sufficient supply of fresh air the breathing is interfered with and asphyxia or suffocation is the result. Unless the cause is speedily removed and the supply of oxygen restored, the paddler will die. Drowning is the most common cause of asphyxia, and can occur wherever there is water — even in inch-deep pools, so never leave an accident victim lying face down in or near water.

Signs and symptoms These vary with the degree of asphyxia present, but in the later stages the following occur:

1. The lips, nose, ears, fingers and toes turn bluish grey.
2. Breathing is intermittent or absent. Pulse is slow and irregular.
3. Complete loss of consciousness.

Treatment Speed is essential to establish a free flow of air to the lungs.

Ensure that the air passage is free from all obstructions and tilt the head back so that expired air resuscitation can commence.

EAR (expired air resuscitation) Support the patient and tilt the head back as far as it will go. Pinch the nose, take a deep breath, cover the patient's mouth with yours, ensuring a good seal, and blow into the patient's lungs. Watch for the chest to rise. Remove your mouth and watch for the patient's chest to fall. At this stage, the lungs should receive a large amount of air, so the initial five to six breaths must be done relatively quickly.

Continue this process until the patient can breath without assistance, or until expert medical aid is available.

External cardiac compression This is now an established and effective method of revival that has saved many lives. The technique involved depends upon the correct compression of the heart between the sternum and vertebral column. (Damage to the ribs is generally unavoidable during the process.)

Procedure

1. The patient must be on his back on a level surface.
2. Kneel at the side of the patient and place the heel of one hand on the lower part of the sternum with the other hand over it. The arms should be straight and the shoulders over the mid-line of the body.
3. A depression of the sternum of approximately 1½ inches is required by adults, and correspondingly less by children. This is to be done at the rate of 60 compressions per minute. (The pressure applied is approximately half the body weight of the patient.)

Drown proofing (sub-surface survival swimming)

The techniques are generally different for men and women, and vary for salt and fresh water, because of the difference in density of the water, and the difference in flotation power in men and women, as well as the existence of natural sinkers. The techniques are designed to produce the best air exchange, and the greatest conservation of energy, utilizing to the full the individual's natural flotation power with air in the lungs.

The movement and rest periods must be light

and relaxed, and this technique provides self protection, as well as a new joy and confidence in the water.

For those concerned with the training of young people, these techniques are a very challenging medium.

The training starts with the immersion of the head in water.

This is to be followed by exhaling through the nose as the head rises from the water, completing the exhalation just as the nose clears the surface. One single breath through the mouth is taken before returning under water. One breath, and only one breath, produces the required balanced air exchange, and complete exhalation is vital to success. Most

56 Men's floating technique in salt water.

a) Rest and relax   b) Ready

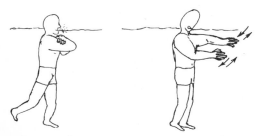

c) Exhale through nose   d) Inhale through mouth — one breath only

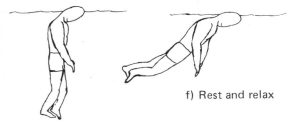

e) Immediately head down, stop sinking with 2nd hand stroke

f) Rest and relax

beginners take in too much air, so try to remember — not too much and not too little. The breathing should be relaxed and rhythmical and not too deep.

It is important to cough and exclude water from the mouth with the head under water.

The individual's natural flotation must be fully exploited, with quiet breathing, light movements and relaxed rest. The aim is to achieve long distance swimming and long period flotation even with cramp or injury, without the use of arms or legs, or indeed both.

Begin with periods of 3 or 4 seconds, which should lengthen to about 10 or 11 as confidence is acquired.

It is important to change your air before you absolutely have to. If you are becoming tight in the chest, gasping, or feeling exhausted, check three vital points: are you taking too big a breath; are you releasing the air in proper exhalation; are you waiting too long before making the air exchange?

Men's floating technique — in salt water Used by approximately 50 per cent of men, i.e. those who do not have high flotation power.

For women and men of equal flotation power, say 50 per cent, it requires only minimal effort to raise the head because of the high flotation of the lower trunk.

Note Positions (b) and (c): Hands to opposite elbow, place arms to forehead while one foot lifts and stands on the water to achieve upright position, breathing out through the nose. Exhalation is completed as the nose comes above water, to be followed by a single intake of air while the arms support the position with one light broad sweep.

Women's technique — (for high floaters) Used by all women and 50 per cent of men in salt water, the men being those with more than the average man's flotation power. In fresh water, all women, and a high proportion of men use this method. Not used by sinkers.

As confidence increases with experience the floater allows his or her natural buoyancy to come more strongly into play. Hand and leg movements become more light and relaxed, with aid from the hands quite unnecessary.

Travel stroke for men and women Float, air exchange and travel series. Women begin exhalation on latter part of glide in both fresh water and salt water. Men exhale on latter part of glide in salt water, on rise of head in fresh water.

Note Exhalation must be in one light, smooth, continuous effort.

All sinkers must use the travel stroke to remain afloat, as they require the momentum of the glide, the time period of which must be reduced to 3 or 4 seconds between positions (h) and (i) in fig. 58.

57 Women's technique — for high floaters.

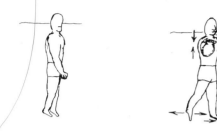

a) Rest

b) Ready

c) Exhale through nose

d) Inhale through mouth — one breath only

e) Arrest sink, hands and feet as required, particularly in fresh water

f) Rest and relax

Forms of rescue

Kayak

Over the years many different forms of rescue have been devised but straightforward methods are always the best. These should be practised so that they become automatic, because in emergencies quick action and knowledge of correct procedures can avert panic. Three simple manoeuvres are the bow rescue, the T rescue and the H rescue. These are easily learnt, are simple to execute and cover most situations.

Bow rescue First and simplest is a bow rescue. This is to help someone who has fallen out of a kayak near a bank or shore and the idea is to get the paddler to hang on to the end of the rescue boat. It makes no difference which end but if it is the bow he should lie flat in the water practically under the boat. If he is hanging on to the stern, he will be trailed along behind. The rescuer should paddle to shore as quickly as possible so that the person in the water can get out and start to get warm. The rescuer may need to go back to help others or, if everyone is safe, to bring back the loose craft. This can be hauled to the bank by attaching the end loop to the end of the rescue boat. Loose equipment can be retrieved next.

The bow rescue is designed to help a paddler who is not injured or dazed in any way and it is particularly useful in a fast flowing river where the paddler in trouble could become wrapped around a rock or swept over a waterfall. See fig. 59.

T rescue The T rescue is an open water rescue for situations where it is impracticable to get the paddler or the boat to shore quickly and where there are only two boats. The paddler who has capsized swims to the side of the rescue kayak holding his overturned craft. It should be upside down and should not have taken in too much water. The man in the water now swims around to the other side of the rescuing craft and rests while the rescuing paddler shakes the water out of the other canoe and manoeuvres it across his own (a). The overturned boat is slowly lifted on to the bow of the rescue craft so that the two boats form a T. Obviously, this needs to be done carefully, with the man in the water helping to stabilize the rescue craft (b). See fig. 60.

Once the boat is out of the water and the water has run out the man still in the water should get back into his kayak. This is not as difficult as it sounds! When the boat is empty it can be turned upright and moved parallel to the rescue craft. The man in the water then grabs the stern of his own kayak and, by pressing down on it, slides himself forward astride it until he can slip into the cockpit. Then he picks up his paddle and is back in business.

H rescue The H rescue is for a situation where there are three or more boats and one capsizes. The two paddlers who are safe come to the ends of the overturned boat, which is presumably upside down and without too much water inside. If there is a fair amount of water inside it will have to be emptied so the paddlers manoeuvre themselves into an H formation, each one holding on to an end of the boat. With a see-saw action, first one end is lifted,

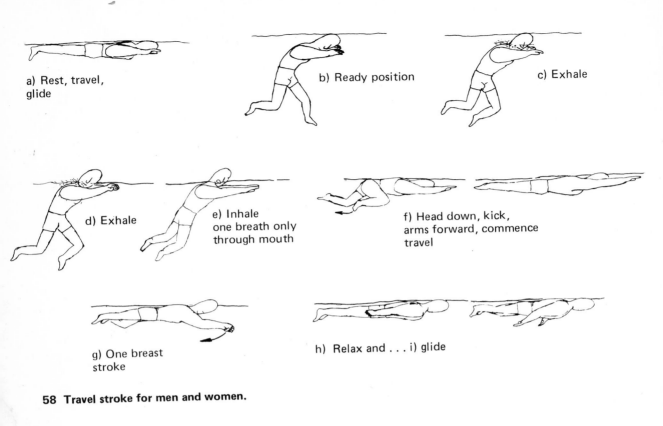

a) Rest, travel, glide

b) Ready position

c) Exhale

d) Exhale

e) Inhale one breath only through mouth

f) Head down, kick, arms forward, commence travel

g) One breast stroke

h) Relax and . . . i) glide

58 Travel stroke for men and women.

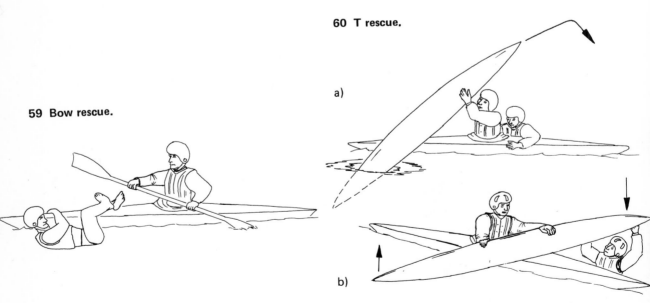

60 T rescue.

a)

59 Bow rescue.

b)

then the other — not both at once. If the capsized boat has taken a lot of water (perhaps because the paddler ignored safety rules and left out buoyancy bags) it would be too heavy to lift. By turning it on one side, most of the water will slowly run out, then the see-saw action can be used.

Meanwhile the paddler of the overturned kayak should move to the stern of one of the rescuing craft while hanging on to his paddle. He can assist by stopping the boats from drifting apart, a real problem since boats going through the rescue procedure tend to be more subject to wind or current. When his kayak is ready, he can clamber over the stern and slip back into the cockpit.

Eskimo bow rescue This is used at sea or in very cold water when the paddler has lost his paddle and is unable to right himself. In these conditions paddlers will not want to come out of their kayaks because of the danger of hypothermia.

Hanging upside down in the water, the paddler puts his hands by his sides, which means that they are sticking out of the water. With one hand he bangs on the hull of the kayak to attract attention while the other is kept high in the air so that his companions can home in on him (a). The rescue boat's

bow should be pushed gently into the palm of the upturned hand. Once there is something to grasp, he can pull himself and his kayak the right way up (b). Even if he goes over again, he will have managed to get a lungful of air. If no one comes immediately, he just has to keep sticking his head up from underneath the water to get some air.

Eventually, if he cannot right himself with a hand roll or if no one comes, he has to get out of his boat. See fig. 62.

This only serves to emphasize that when on open water, paddlers must keep each other in sight all the time and stay aware of what each is doing.

Canoe

The rescue methods for kayaks are also used for canoes. Since there are usually two men in an open canoe, it is easier to perform these manoeuvres, particularly the T rescue. With two men in the rescue boat, one pulls the bow of the overturned boat up and over the boat while his companion keeps their canoe steady by leaning his weight the other way. The capsized canoe is then turned the right way up and put back in the water. The two boats are rafted up together and the paddler in the water clambers

61 H rescue.

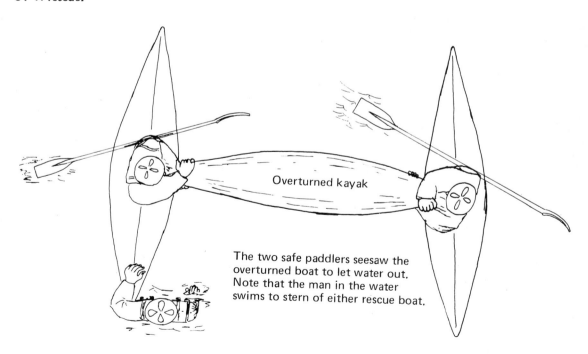

Overturned kayak

The two safe paddlers seesaw the overturned boat to let water out. Note that the man in the water swims to stern of either rescue boat.

back into his boat from the far side. Paddles are used to give the boats stability. This operation is also made easier because canoes are open, so the water is not trapped in the deck, it just flows out.

Sometimes a capsize accident happens when the paddler seems to be ejected from the boat. He falls over the side but the boat does not turn over. In this case the canoeist can get back into the open canoe just by getting hold of one end of the boat and pulling himself up on to what there is of the deck before clambering in. It takes some practice but it is quite feasible.

Whatever the rescue method, the swimmer should always hang on to the rescue boat because even the slightest breeze can make the boats drift sideways at quite a speed.

62 Eskimo bow rescue.

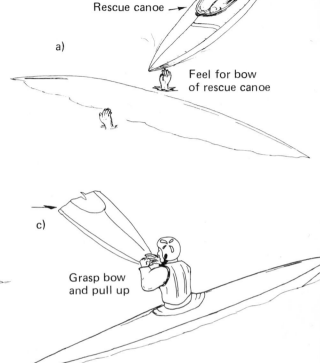

a)

Rescue canoe

Feel for bow of rescue canoe

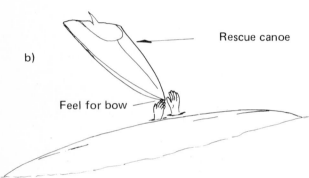

b)

Rescue canoe

Feel for bow

c)

Grasp bow and pull up

CHAPTER 6
Fitness for Competition

Research has shown that kayak and canoe paddlers who reach international championship levels have usually come into the sport between the ages of 12 and 14. Nineteen and 20 year olds have appeared for the past number of years amongst the European, World and Olympic medallists in both kayak and canoe events. This pattern will continue, so it is necessary for young people to acquire technique, tactics and general all-round physiological development before they are 18. Then, and only then, when their bones have virtually stopped growing, should they start strenuous specific strength and power training. If serious training, particularly with weights, is attempted any earlier there is a chance of inflicting permanent damage on the paddler which might not manifest itself until years later, by which time the person and occasions responsible will have been forgotten.

Research over the past ten years has indicated that achievements by 18 and 19 year olds are not the result of strength and power training but rather of mental rehearsal, technique and general all-round physical education. The unpredictable pattern of competitive results in this age group, it would seem, comes from subjecting immature physiques to a high degree of strain. With the onset of physical maturation, generally between 20 and 22, results steadily become more consistent and the champions, whose hallmark is consistency, emerge. When planning fitness training schedules the reasons must be considered.

A paddler may feel very fit and yet when he gets on the water, he drops right out of the back of a race. One or two simple scientific tests might have proved to him that, in purely physiological paddling terms, he was far from fit. It should be noted that it is also possible to be efficiently fit for one sport, but wholly unfit and totally unsuited for another.

The criteria for all fitness training dictates that it must relate to a specific sport and, especially at competitive or elite level, to a particular individual — the aspect of individually trained regimes is all too often ignored.

Canoeing demands more endurance than most sports and therefore it is necessary to look at a number of physiological factors that are brought into play in paddling. There are three areas of physical efficiency recognized by most coaches — cardio-vascular efficiency, local muscular efficiency and anaerobic efficiency. There is no particular significance in this order.

In order to maintain effective paddling over a long period, oxygen must be supplied to the larger groups of working muscles. This requires heart and lung endurance (cardio-vascular).

Local muscular endurance implies the ability to use local muscle groups for long periods of time without the paddler having to experience anything more than slight tiredness. Canoeing is demanding of most muscle groups in the body but particularly of back, shoulder and arm muscles. These must be submitted, having regard to age and physical type, to high levels of training in both the kayak and the canoe and in other activities such as special weight training exercises, swimming and skiing in order to develop that high level of endurance.

Anaerobic, in simple terms, refers to working without much oxygen; 'aerobic' refers to there being sufficient oxygen to carry out the activity. In general terms this is the difference between the 500-metre sprint race (mostly anaerobic) and the 10,000-metre race (aerobic). In fact, athletes' muscles are suited more to one event than to another. As a report in the *New York Times* explained in August 1980, muscles are made up of two types of fibre, fast-twitch and slow-twitch. These are familiar to most people as the light and dark meat of chicken or turkey.

The fast-twitch muscle fibres contract rapidly and can produce bursts of power at high speeds but tire rather quickly. Slow-twitch fibres, on the other hand, contract more slowly and with less power but can keep going for a long time.

The average person has a 50-50 distribution of slow- and fast-twitch fibres in major skeletal muscles. A similar ratio is likely to be found in weight lifters, shot-putters and high jumpers. But the muscles of long-distance runners and swimmers

63 The DDR team performing pre-event stretching exercises under the supervision of DDR coach Wolf Dieter.

average about 80 per cent slow-twitch fibres whereas sprinters average more than 75 per cent fast-twitch fibres.

The different fibre types rely on somewhat different energy sources. As Dr Robert Arnot, Director of the Sports Medicine Centre at Lake Placid, New York, noted: the chicken wing tastes sweet because fast-twitch fibres use glycogen (stored sugar) for energy, whereas the leg has more fat because slow-twitch fibres are fuelled by fatty acids as well as glycogen.

Slow-twitch fibres are aerobic; that is, they use oxygen to burn fuel. Their red colour is due to myoglobin, the pigment that supplies muscle cells with oxygen (the way haemoglobin carries oxygen to the blood). The endurance of slow-twitch fibres is limited by their fuel supply which ordinarily runs out after about two hours of moderately strenuous activity, such as jogging. This is what happens when a kayak marathoner 'hits the wall' — reaches a point of exhaustion — at around 15 to 20 miles.

Fast-twitch fibres are more likely to work anaerobically, without oxygen, with fatigue resulting from the build-up of lactic acid, which prevents the muscles from generating more energy.

Studies of human muscle fibre types have shown that the percentage of slow-twitch and fast-twitch fibres in one's muscles is genetically determined; the basic type cannot be changed by the kind of exercise done.

But changes in the metabolic properties of the fibres are possible. The slow- and fast-twitch fibres are used differently in different activities and are affected differently by training techniques. Extensive endurance-type training can cause fast-twitch fibres to behave more like slow-twitch ones, although the reverse does not occur following the power or speed training such as weight lifting or sprinting.

. . . Research . . . has shown that endurance training, such as through jogging or swimming laps, increases the size and efficiency of slow-twitch fibres. Both the number of mitochondria, which are the respiratory powerhouses of a cell, and the amount of enzymes that burn fuel in the presence of oxygen increase as a result of endurance training. Furthermore, endurance-type activities increase the number of capilliaries surrounding a muscle fibre, enabling it to obtain more oxygen, fuel and nutrients. The net result is a more efficient muscle cell that burns more fatty acids, sparing the limited supply of glycogen and delaying fatigue.

Strength may be looked at, simply, in two distinct

parts: dynamic and static strength. Static strength is the capacity to exert force for short periods against an immovable object. On its own, this type of training has no place in kayaking or canoeing but, together with dynamic strength (the capacity to move an object), it is important in the generation of power — and this is of tremendous value in canoe sport.

Suppleness (flexibility or mobility) is neglected by most paddlers and yet is an essential element of fitness for canoe sport. It is the ability to move various parts of the body, such as the trunk and limbs, through a wide range of movements.

Paediatricians state that a child is born with a high degree of mobility — a new born baby can bend backwards, head almost touching feet, without harm. Unfortunately, this mobility disappears with the advance of years and the acquisition of increased muscle bulk.

Mobility depends upon the flexibility of the joints. These have an in-built warning system which flashes a caution to the central nervous system when maximum movement has been reached. The cautionary system can, in the case of an athlete, be somewhat over-protective and so it is necessary during training to stretch joints almost to the maximum. (A list of useful stretching exercises is given below.)

Cardio-vascular efficiency is dependent upon a strong heart and its efficiency can be developed by going for long runs which should be in excess of 20 minutes. The heart needs to be worked very hard (which is what exercise physiologists call 'sustained overload') in order to make it adapt. The runs may be modified by running at varying speeds during a particular session — a practice called 'fartleck running'.

In local muscular endurance training it is unnecessary to raise the heart rate to the levels demanded in other forms of training. A circuit of exercises involving double knee jumps, burpees, squat thrusts, pull-ups, sit-ups, push-ups, dips and 'pattering' (fast sprinting on the spot) is an ideal way of developing specific muscles. In most programmes, the athlete would complete the 'circuit' three times. The number of repetitions is increased as the athlete builds up his endurance.

Training to improve anaerobic efficiency alternates very hard work with a break or rest period. This is often referred to as 'intermittent work'; interval training is the most common form. Interval training (on land) consists of running very fast for, say, 50 yards, then jogging for 150 yards. This is repeated a number of times. The pulse rate should increase to at least 180 b.p.m. possibly more, drop-ping to 130 b.p.m. during the rest periods.

The search for speed is an essential ingredient of all training and an analysis of current trends in speed training indicates that most training in Eastern Europe and now increasingly elsewhere emphasizes the arms in speed routines.

One such method for canoeists is flat-out hitting (using both arms) of a punch bag at the rate of 70 to 80 hits a minute using a variety of routines. It has been argued that 'this develops in the canoeist rhythm, power and relaxation.'

Another important point is to avoid the use of training over long distances. Therefore, apart from the pre-season build-up of time on the water, the early competitive season training should accentuate short-distance work. So, mileage early on, short distances later.

In the immediate pre-competition build-up every aspect of training should be done 'flat out'. It is said that 'If you want to go faster, react faster, think faster, then you must go faster, react faster, think faster!!'

A recently completed study of both Western and Eastern European paddlers has indicated that a number of individual and team sports can be used in off-water and in out-of-season training routines. Swimming, basketball and volley-ball are popular, whilst in snowy regions the effect of langlauf or cross-country skiing is also beneficial — there is an established and marked correlation between skiing and canoeing.

Suppleness is best achieved by establishing an individual routine, involving a full range of movements, An athlete must remember not to 'bounce' into the exercises — rather should he press into each movement. The following exercises have been well tested and may be used in their own right or for warming-up before an event.

1. Calf stretch Face a wall and support yourself against it. Keep feet together and both legs straight with heels maintaining contact with floor. Slowly press hips forward to stretch calf muscle.

2. Achilles and lower calf stretch Adopt similar position to (1), but place one foot forward. Keeping weight on rear leg and heel on floor, allow both knees to bend until stretching sensation is felt in lower calf.

3. Hip rotation Adopt same starting position as (2) with one leg forward. Slowly press hip of rear leg to side and hold. Repeat for other hip.

4. Adductor stretch Stand with feet very wide apart and hands on hips. Keep right leg straight and sway to left as left knee bends. Lean sideways over straight leg until stretching sensation is felt inside upper thigh. Repeat to opposite side.

5. Lower back and hamstring stretch Lie on your back. Slowly raise legs above your head keeping knees lightly bent. As your hips leave mat support them with your hands. Relax, breathe normally and hold. Eventually learn to keep legs straight for maximum benefit.

6. Side stretch Join the arms overhead and bend slowly sideways at the waist, not pressing too hard. Hold. Repeat for other side.

7. Trunk rotation Stand with feet shoulder-width apart and fingers clasped in front of chest with elbows pointing sideways. Keeping feet fixed, turn head and whole body to side as far as possible, then press further. Repeat to other side.

8. Quadriceps stretch Support yourself with left hand against wall. Grasp right ankle with right hand, bend knee and draw back as far as possible behind hip keeping upper body vertical. Repeat to other side.

9. Hamstring stretch From comfortable standing position bend forward from hips keeping legs and back straight and let arms hang loosely. A stretching sensation will be felt behind thighs. *Do not bounce.* Relax through the tension. Hold.

10. Hurdler's stretch (for hamstrings, adductors and quadriceps). Adopt hurdling position on mat. a) Clasp underside of knee with both hands and lean forward attempting to touch knee with forehead. b) Lean backwards towards rear foot supporting weight on hands behind body.

11. Upper hamstring and hip stretch Lie on back. Keeping right leg straight, lift left leg, clasp it and pull it towards chest. Aim to keep head in contact with mat. Repeat to other side.

12. Quadriceps, calf and hip stretch Adopt deep forward lunge position with rear toe on floor and pointing forward. Lean back from waist and press hips downwards until stretching sensation is felt. Hold.

Fig. 64 illustrates the protection afforded to the joint by the ligaments which, as well as forming a connection between two joints, also prevent the bones from drifting too far out of line. If the ligaments become loose and ineffective then there is a chance of the bones becoming damaged and the cartilage worn until it reaches a condition in which it is vulnerable and might tear. This is a state that precedes the onset of arthritis.

The muscles and their associated tendons also play an important part in the protection of the joint and, if they are maintained in good condition, are able to fulfil, more easily, their protective functions.

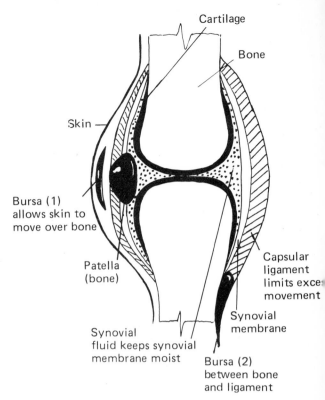

64 Stylized drawing of joint.

These points are made to illustrate the value to be obtained from following a routine of simple stretching exercises.

Team paddling is a variation on the theme of interval paddling. Four or five canoeists from the same club or team go on the water together with each taking it in turn to be 'coach'. The 'coach' then designates the finishing line — e.g. the boat house on the left or the second telegraph pole and gets his colleagues to sprint away having given a 'Ready, steady, go!' This routine should be followed by a steady-rate period of paddling whilst the group reform and the winner takes up his position as the next 'coach'.

Another 'fun' alternative is 'hare and hounds', with the slower members being given a start in the race to the finishing line.

Training programmes should be tailored to the individual, as should training plans.

The aim of a training programme is to produce a maximum peak performance at a number of specific times during the racing season. Prior to initiating or structuring the programme, it is vital to consider the pattern of the whole competitive season and the specific competitions or events in which the canoeist will compete. The timings of selection events or international competitions are particularly critical. The nature and pattern of the competitive season will therefore dictate the pattern of the training plan.

Training for general aerobic fitness, on the water, is achieved by sustained steady-rate paddling for long stretches of time. This is particularly relevant to marathon canoeists.

Training for anaerobic fitness, on the water, is best achieved by interval paddling along the lines of the following schedules which should be modified and adapted to individual routines.

It has to be remembered that the differing disciplines, within the sport of canoeing, require differing degrees of strength and endurance. As an example, the slalom paddler requires strength, but requires less endurance than, say, the marathon paddler.

Anaerobic training — Session 1

1500 m warm-up, including 4 x 50-stroke burns (very fast paddling) — (counting on both sides).
8 x split 1000 m of 4 x 100 strokes.
At least 3 minutes' rest between each of the split 1000 m and a 50-stroke rest between each of the 100-stroke work periods.
1000 m warm-down, concentrating on technique and relaxed paddling.

Anaerobic training — Session 2

1500 m warm-up, including 5 x 40-stroke burns — (counting on both sides).
11 x split 500 m of 4 x 500 strokes.
At least 3 minutes between each of the split 500 m and a 40-stroke rest between each of the 50-stroke work periods.
3 x 50-stroke starts (rolling), 50-stroke rest.
3 x 50-stroke starts (standing), 50-stroke rest, kayak stationary.
1000 m warm-down, concentrating on technique and paddling relaxed.

Anaerobic training — Session 3

1500 m warm-up, including 10 x 20-stroke burns — (counting both sides).
4 x 20 strokes effort, 40 strokes rest.
4 x 40 strokes effort, 60 strokes rest.
4 x 60 strokes effort, 60 strokes rest.
4 x 40 strokes effort, 60 strokes rest.
4 x 20 strokes effort, 40 strokes rest.
1000 m relaxed, light paddling.
4 x 20 strokes effort, 40 strokes rest.

4 x 40 strokes effort, 60 strokes rest.
4 x 60 strokes effort, 60 strokes rest.
4 x 40 strokes effort, 60 strokes rest.
4 x 20 strokes effort, 40 strokes rest.
1000 m warm-down, concentrating on technique and relaxed paddling.

Anaerobic training — Session 4

1500 m warm-up, including 8 x 30-stroke burns — (counting both sides).
10 x 20 strokes effort, 40 strokes rest.
 6 x 40 strokes effort, 60 strokes rest.
 4 x 60 strokes effort, 60 strokes rest.
 2 x 80 strokes effort, 80 strokes rest.
 1 x 100 strokes effort, 100 strokes rest.
 2 x 80 strokes effort, 80 strokes rest.
 4 x 60 strokes effort, 60 strokes rest.
 6 x 40 strokes effort, 60 strokes rest.
10 x 20 strokes effort, 40 strokes rest.
1000 m warm-down, concentrating on technique and relaxed paddling.

Anaerobic training — Session 5

1500 m warm-up, including 5 x 40-stroke burns — (counting on both sides).
8 x 20 strokes effort, 40 strokes rest.
1000 m relaxed, light paddling.
4 x 40 strokes effort, 60 strokes rest.
1000 m relaxed, light paddling.
8 x 20 strokes effort, 40 strokes rest.
1000 m relaxed, light paddling.
5 x 50 stroke starts (rolling), 50 stroke rest.
5 x 50 stroke starts (standing), 50 stroke rest.
1000 m warm-down, concentrating on technique and paddling relaxed.

The following schematic graph on pages 66-67 illustrates the training plan for a European marathon paddler. This graph is the actual projection of a British paddler for a European international season. It is interesting to note that there is a programmed transitional period between each type of training which allows for physiological adaptation and which in turn helps to avoid strain. It is also of interest to note the careful selection of competitions, selection events and major internationals all leading to what British paddlers see as the premier event (The Gudena Marathon — the unofficial world championships).

There is no particular routine or series of routines that will suit every paddler. The planned routine, for each phase of the year, will alter from individual to individual according to time, finance, climate, available water, multi-gyms, etc. Programmes will

65

also differ according to the particular canoe discipline and geographical location and must be the decision of individual coaches.

It is quite impossible to over-emphasize the value of training logs or motivation sheets though many paddlers, particularly those who train themselves outside a squad, seem reluctant to adopt the practice — arguing that it is 'time wasted that can be spent on training!' Lessons are learned from 'history' and it is of inestimable value to look back at competitive results and related training and preparation.

A log, or series of motivation sheets, helps to maintain progress and is an invaluable reference when approaching the compilation of next season's training programme.

Useful information for inclusion in a log are:
1. On-water schedules
2. Weight training schedules
3. Length of sessions
4. State of health
5. Pulse rate
6. Weight
7. Race results — positions of major opponents
8. Relationship with management (manager/coach)

The following is an example of a motivation sheet that might be adapted to suit any individual competing in any canoeing discipline.

MOTIVATION SHEET

WEEK NUMBER ——————— DATE WEEK COMMENCED ————————————————

Total mileage (paddling) ————————————
Total mileage (running) ————————————
Total mileage for the week (paddling) ——————
Total mileage for the week (running) —————
Percentage of boat training in ————————
— K1 ————————— —K2 —————————
— RR ———————— —Slalom —————————

General Comments ————————————————
————————————————————————————————
————————————————————————————————
————————————————————————————————
————————————————————————————————
————————————————————————————————
————————————————————————————————

TIME TRIALS
Distance ————————————————————
Type of boat ————————————————————
Times ————————————————————
Appetite ————————————————————
Sleep ————————————————————
Weight ————————————————————
Resting pulse ————————————————————

	Session 1	Session 2	Session 3	Running	WT	CT
Mon.						
Tues.						
Wed.						
Thur.						
Fri.						
Sat.						
Sun.						
Total						

Waterside series
A   B   C   D

Exe descent
17 miles

Light weight training
and circuit training

19 miles   35 miles
15 miles   23 miles

Heavy weight
training period

October ——————— December   January ——————— March

Transition to heavy weight training
— strength and power

Transition period from
heavy to light weight
training

Transition from light
weights to greater
paddling distance w

General exercises and weight training

Schedules, as already stated, should be tailored to the individual athlete and records of progress kept. Before structuring a schedule, it is necessary to ascertain a paddler's capacity (maximum) and then work a training routine that involves using a weight or number of repetitions that approximate two-thirds of maximum. Individual exercises for strength should be carried out for approximately one minute or a maximum of 30 repetitions. There is room for much individual training and again, at the highest levels, it is absolutely necessary for paddlers to have expert supervision with individually assessed and tailored regimes.

Circuit training schedules should be considered to develop strength and general cardio-vascular efficiency.

Caution: It is advisable to concentrate, in earlier schedules, on trunk strengthening exercises in order to avoid backache problems.

Exercises must be adjusted according to facilities and equipment available. The following standard, much used, exercises are not exhaustive but are a general guide (fig. 65):

a) Upward punching. This is an alternate upward punching routine using dumb-bells.

b) Forward punching. Alternate forward punching action using dumb-bells. Keep arms horizontal to the ground.

c) Side flexing. Side flexing action to alternate sides with dumb-bells. The weight on the opposite side to that which is bending is pulled up as far as possible under the armpit.

d) Bent-over rowing with rotation. The weights are pulled up to alternate shoulders with a rotation trunk.

e) Small circles. The palms of the hands face upwards and the circles made should be very small.

f) Chin-ups. On ropes, rings or beam.

g) Standing press. From chest height raise weights full above head.

h) Bent-over rowing. Raise weights to chest with head supported (it strengthens arms and shoulders).

i) Curls. Feet apart. Weight held at arms length. Palms forward from below bar. Weight lifted to chest.

j) Bench-press. Lay on back — weight on chest. Push weight up. An inclined bench may be used.

k) Press-ups. Very effective if feet raised about 12 inches from floor.

l) Sit-ups. Very effective if trunk is turned (rotated) during sit-up so elbow reaches outside opposite knee.

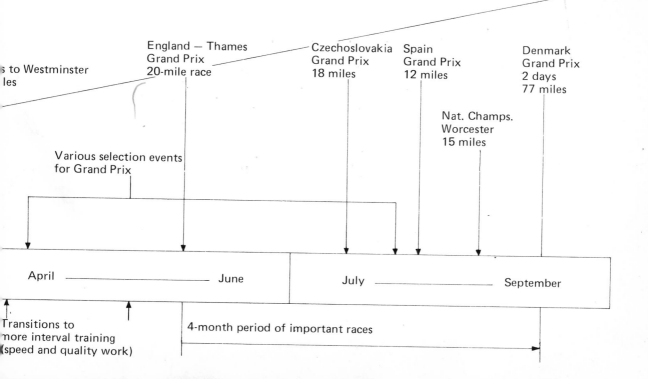

m) Back-curls. Face down on bench weights behind neck. Raise trunk and arch back.

n) Kayak rotation. Kayak sitting position with weights behind neck. Rotate trunk from side to side.

Pre-event diet and special diets

In this particular area of sports training there are a lot of non-controlled, pseudo-scientific recommendations. Paddlers are no exception when it comes to trying unscientific 'fad' diets. One example is the marathon paddler who, on the day of an event has only black coffee and four Mars bars for breakfast, arguing that he would be unable to perform well on any other breakfast regime. Then there is the sprint paddler who always eats two or three small packets of dates and brown bread. On the day someone ate

65 Exercises.

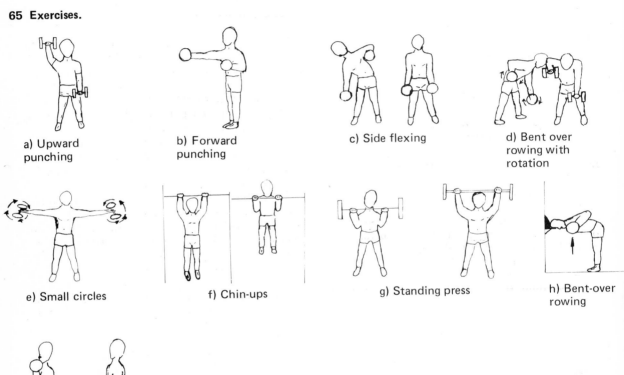

a) Upward punching

b) Forward punching

c) Side flexing

d) Bent over rowing with rotation

e) Small circles

f) Chin-ups

g) Standing press

h) Bent-over rowing

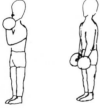

i) Curls

j) Bench press

k) Press-ups

l) Sit-ups

m) Back curls

n) Kayak rotation

his dates, he refused to paddle! These paddlers are symptomatic of the confused and uninformed way in which many prepare themselves for competition.

Another common affliction amongst many aspiring canoeists and kayakers has been the tendency to seek a 'magic potion', bottled, packaged or home-made, which guarantees competitive success. The most recent is the glyceride depletion diet. It hides itself under a cloud of jargon and fancy names — viz 'Glycogen Boost Diet', 'Carbohydrate Bleed-Out Diet', 'Carbohydrate Booster', 'Glucose Reserve Diet' or simply 'The Diet'.

The confusion about this particular diet is a result of work undertaken by Dr Bengt Saltin, physiologist at the August Krogh Institute in Copenhagen. The trouble is that coaches have merely implemented non-controlled and non-standardized versions of his work without proper study and research.

Dr Saltin's research was based on a glyceride depletion diet with marathon runners. The common factor in all the versions of the diet is the depletion of the glycogen reserves (stored sugar) within the body. This was a result of vigorous running and exercises during which period the athlete avoided totally, or almost, carbohydrate-loaded or fat-loaded foods and relied solely, or as near as possible, on protein as the main energy source. Just before the competition the depleted glycogen reserves are replenished by rest and carbohydrate-rich foods.

The well-known British coach, Wilf Paish, sets out successfully the underlying principles behind carbohydrate loading:

During prolonged exercise, the carbohydrate reserves of the body are depleted. Energy for exercise is derived almost entirely from the metabolism of fats and carbohydrates. Whereas the reserve supply of fats is almost inexhaustible, carbohydrates are only stored in limited amounts.

Once the carbohydrate supplies have been depleted, fats are used for energy. However, when fats are used for energy the efficiency of the body is reduced; which must be reflected in a reduction of training/competition times.

The rate at which glycogen is depleted depends upon the intensity of the work load. At very high levels of work the body obtains a greater proportion of its energy from carbohydrates.

The only way to obtain a complete depletion of glycogen is to exercise at an intense level so that muscle and liver glycogen stores are expended. Without depletion of glycogen, extra carbohydrates will not produce the over-compensated effect.

Depletion is necessary in order to stimulate fully the enzymic activity necessary for the synthesis of glycogen.

During the depletion phase, some carbohydrates are necessary in order to facilitate the correct functioning of several important systems, for example, kidneys, nervous system and red blood cell production. Likewise, during the loading phase, some protein is essential for tissue repair.

During the loading phase, extra fluids must be consumed as a certain proportion of water is stored with each unit of glycogen. If the fluid intake is not increased, other body fluids will be used, which could lead to a relative condition of dehydration.

For over-compensation to take place, there must be a relative period of rest during the loading phase. Hence, this must be allowed for in the eating process, otherwise it would be possible to overeat and so affect the strength/weight ratio.

The precise peaking effect will vary from person to person. Usually, the peak will occur between two and four days from the loading period. However, it is important to experiment before the all-important occasion, to make sure that the maximum benefit from the system has been achieved.

Many top-class marathon runners have experimented with the diet, as advocated by Saltin, and some have had considerable success. Saltin, in his original work, claimed a difference of seven minutes, over a 30-kilometre run, in favour of those who used the loading diet. Other research workers in the United States have supported these findings. The most marked effect is over the final stages of a run, when normal glycogen supplies would be very low.

The total system would appear to be as follows:
1. Seven days before the big event, the competitor takes a fast, sustained run of about 30 kilometres to deplete the glycogen stores.

2. For the next three days he continues training on an almost carbohydrate-free diet.

3. For the remaining three days, including the day of the competition, he loads with carbohydrates.

Paish reported that 'in conversation with athletes who have used this system, the problem which emerges appears to be the "low" feeling during the depletion phase, while training is continued. Some have suggested that it could shatter an athlete's confidence unless he has complete faith in the system.'

From personal experience of athletes taking part in the Gudena Kayak Marathon in Denmark it was clear that there were, in some cases, a number of worrying side effects. Possibly the most serious was the case of a junior paddler who had undertaken a so-called diet without any qualified supervision and was depressed to a state that should have caused concern.

Recently a number of athletes have been experimenting with a modified version of the Saltin diet. They are using the depletion run followed immediately by the loading phase, without the three day glyceride depletion period. A number of informed physiologists have suggested that, 'It should be as successful as the earlier method.'

A research physiologist has recently made the following observations:

1. To adhere strictly to the type of dietary regime recommended by Saltin and Hermansen is both boring and expensive. The attractiveness and palatability of foods is a result of mixing protein, fat and carbohydrate in the right proportions.
2. The stimulation of the appropriate enzyme activity in the muscles or liver to increase the amount of glycogen stored over and above normal considerations is very dependent upon the depletion of these stores by strenuous exercise to *exhaustion* and assessment of exhaustion, in the physiological sense, can only be made with the appropriate laboratory facilities. Thus, if this objective is not achieved, it is possible that the glycogen levels will not be significantly greater than normal and the full value will not be derived from this type of diet.
3. Athletes who have used this type of regime often comment upon a 'heavy feeling' in their muscles and those who have used it would not use it more than one or two occasions in their careers, for a very special occasion.
4. I am not alone in the opinion that equally satisfactory results can be achieved by the application of a good training programme together with a balanced diet which could include a liquid dietary supplement (Accolade or Dynamo etc.) when the calorific intake has to be increased. Of course, many users have found liquid supplements to be of considerable value post event, when exhaustion is setting in; glycogen control diets will be of no use in such a situation and the comment is frequently made that exhaustion seems to be worse after such a diet.

These views may not be popular with the protagonists of a glycogen control diet but perhaps they will further stimulate discussion amongst paddlers.

There are a number of well-proven, well-established practices in pre-event eating.

The body stores energy in the form of glycerides and so it is only necessary to supplement during the period before the competition. The supplement should be rich in energy-promoting factors and be easy to digest, which means that it will probably be made up mainly of carbohydrates.

It is essential that adequate time be allowed for the digestion and assimilation of whatever food the paddler may eat, and it is therefore strongly advised that any pre-event food should be taken at least three to four hours before his event is due to start. The most horrendous story is that recounted to a BBC interviewer by a British Davis Cup tennis player in June 1980. He confessed to 'feeling heavy in the legs' during a game and thought it was due to a 'mixed grill' (bacon, sausages, kidneys, chop) he had had less than one hour before his match!

Whereas carbohydrates are easily assimilated, and might well be absorbed in under two hours, proteins in the form of fried fish, steak, or mixed grill will almost certainly take over three hours.

Just before an event it is most common for athletes to lose their appetite and this is almost certainly a direct result of adrenalin secretion — the 'aggression' hormone which helps to improve an athlete's performance in competition, as opposed to training. Some researchers have suggested that a meal eaten at just the right time before an event could delay the secretion of adrenalin until nearer the start time — with obvious beneficial effects in terms of an athlete not becoming psychologically exhausted before he goes on the water.

There are a number of easily digested products on the market (such as Complan) which competitors might experiment with but a simple meal used by a number of Eastern European paddlers might be usefully copied. It consists of ripe, mashed bananas mixed with honey and spread on black or brown bread. The meal is eaten slowly, well chewed and is accompanied by sweet coffee. Some outstanding international and Olympic canoe/kayak gold medal winners use this diet — what more can be said!

Isometric training without equipment

There is some evidence to justify the use of isometric exercise in strength training programmes. Isometric work is also of value in the absence of formal weight training facilities and many paddlers, worldwide, are not able to obtain facilities or afford equipment. Dr Henry Rek of The Polish Canoe Federation has undertaken much research on the subject, and in a published paper justifies use of isometric exercises because they do not require any equipment. The 'role' of the equipment is replaced by the 'antagonistic' muscles.

Dr Rek recommends that the exercises, shown in

1977 Projection of competition and training programme

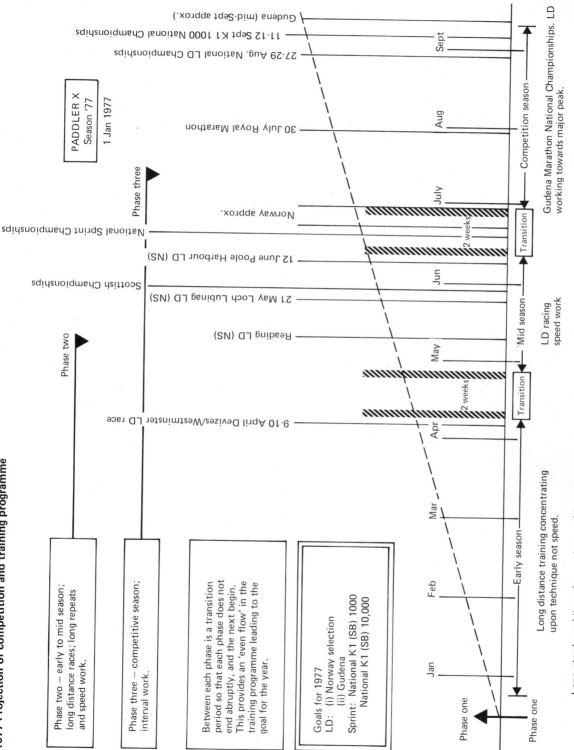

Phase two – early to mid season; long distance races; long repeats and speed work.

Phase three – competitive season; interval work.

Between each phase is a transition period so that each phase does not end abruptly, and the next begin. This provides an 'even flow' in the training programme leading to the goal for the year.

Goals for 1977
LD: (i) Norway selection
     (ii) Gudena
Sprint: National K1 (SB) 1000
        National K1 (SB) 10,000

PADDLER X
Season '77
1 Jan 1977

Phase three

Phase two

Phase one

National Sprint Championships

Scottish Championships

9-10 April Devizes/Westminster LD race

Reading LD (NS)

21 May Loch Lubnag LD (NS)

12 June Poole Harbour LD (NS)

Norway approx.

30 July Royal Marathon

27-29 Aug. National LD Championships

11-12 Sept K1 1000 National Championships

Gudena (mid-Sept. approx.)

Jan   Feb   Mar   Apr   May   Jun   July   Aug   Sept

Phase one

Early season

Mid season

Competition season

Transition   2 weeks   Transition   2 weeks

Long distance training concentrating upon technique not speed.

LD racing speed work

Gudena Marathon National Championships. LD working towards major peak.

Long, steady paddling. Accumulation of large kilometre base.

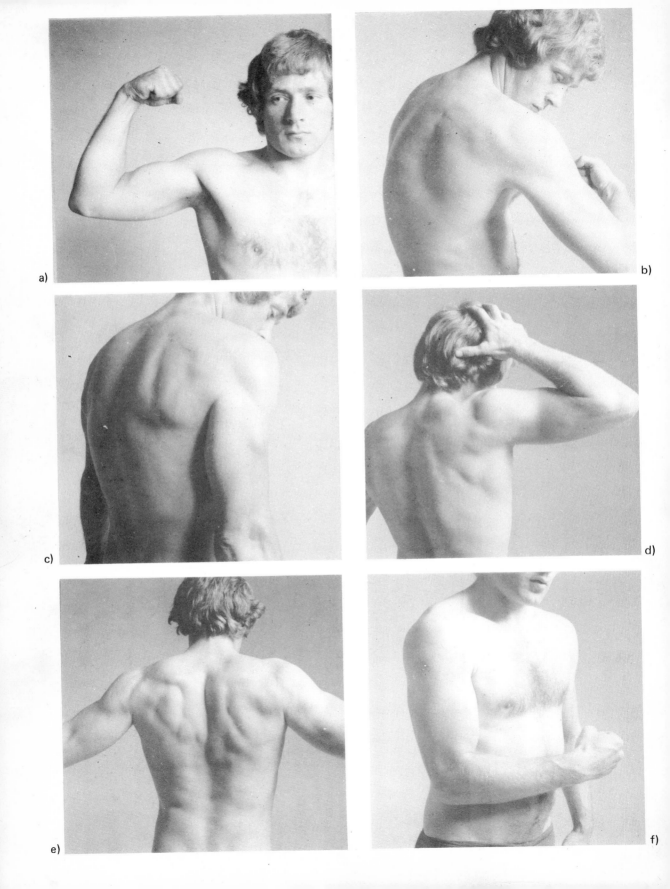

a)

b)

c)

d)

e)

f)

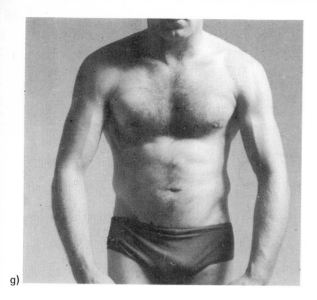

g)

66 Isometric training without equipment.

fig. 66 should be done in series, each exercise lasting 10 to 15 seconds and repeated two or three times. The rest period between each series should be approximately two minutes and the rest between each exercise should be about 30 seconds.

a) The arm is held out at right angles to the body and slightly forward with the elbow bent and the fist clenched. In this position all the muscles of the arm are brought into action.

b) The arm is held down at the side of the body bending slightly to the side of the exercising muscles. This exercises the latissimus tissues.

c) The arm is lowered to the side of the body and straightened. This exercises all the exterior muscles of the arm.

d) The arm is bent at the elbow and raised at the shoulder so that the hand almost comes above the level of the shoulder. This exercises the deltoid muscles and triceps.

e) The arms are stretched to either side with the elbows slightly to the rear. The shoulders should be brought towards one another. This exercises the dorsum, trapesius and synergetic muscles.

f) The trunk is slightly bent forward, with the arms lowered and pressed hard against the body. This exercises the pectoralis major and minor.

g) The trunk is bent forward to exercise the trunk flexor muscles.

For the maximum effect from these exercises Rek considers that they should be done with the maximum of effort, causing muscular pain and possibly cramp.

To help strengthen and stretch the muscle, while the muscles are still working antagonistically, the limb or part of the body can be moved very slowly.

The advantages of these exercises is that they can be done anywhere, at almost any time and in any type of dress. There is no need for special equipment or special clothing.

CHAPTER 7
Racing Competitions: Sprint, Slalom, Wild Water and Marathon

Once paddlers have become competent, there comes a fork in the road. Having learnt all about the different techniques of handling both canoes and kayaks, they enjoy using them for fun, for pleasure or perhaps in small competitions run by clubs. But there comes a point where paddlers think they are really good at the sport and want to follow it seriously. There are plenty of options open to them.

They can do sprint racing, which is flat water racing, or slalom, down a river over a measured distance manoeuvring between poles. They can do wild water racing, which is going down the same sort of river but the intention is to get from A to B as quickly as possible, negotiating only natural obstacles. They can go for marathon racing, which is distances in excess of 10,000 metres ranging from 12 miles right up to the exceptional marathon races lasting a couple of days. They can surf canoe, they can play canoe polo or go canoe sailing. Those are the competitive elements. The ideal age to start is around 13 but it is not too late even after that because early on, strength and determination are more important than skill. People who have later turned out to be great international paddlers have in their early days spent more time in water than in the canoe! So it is strength that comes initially rather than skill.

The 13 year old would be a good athletic build for his age, with broad shoulders and good bone structure — the typical mesamorph. There are exceptions, like the lanky paddlers or the short fat ones, but the real champions come from the well-proportioned athletic type through to the lanky end of the scale. There are no great champions who have come from the other end of the physical scale — the round overtly endomorph. The canoeist is in the same bracket as the modern pentathlon and decathlon athlete. Of all competitive sports worldwide canoeists at the highest international level tend to have the best all-round physical development.

Paddlers tend to be 'lone wolves' and this creates problems at the higher competitive levels when there has to be a relationship between the coach and the coached, the coached and the manager and between the coached and the rest of the team. In other words, the athlete has to relate to the manager, with the coaches and with other team members. Canoeists, by nature, are very individualistic. Over the past few years a number of physical education researchers have carried out personality factor indice tests on groups of international canoeists and found that they tended to have 'bohemian characteristics'.

What is more, aggression is an important factor in all the canoeing events. It shows itself in different ways in the various events. In wild water, for instance, the paddler has to hit that water and drive down river as fast as he can. He's out to beat the river. In marathon racing, it's aggression from the word 'go', because competitors have to fight to get to the front of the bunch and they have to fight to

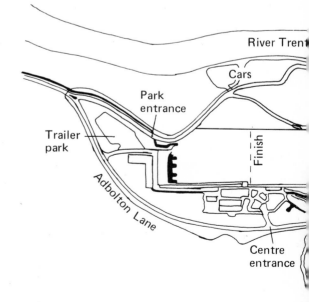

get people off their wash. They have to fight to get past opponents — it is a fight all the way.

Sprint (paddle racing)

Under ICF rules there are no mixed competitions involving either men and women in the same boat or in competition with one another.

The classes with their specifications are as follows:

	Max. length	Min. beam	Min. weight
K1	520 cm	51 cm	12 kg
K2	650 cm	55 cm	18 kg
K4	1100 cm	60 cm	30 kg
C1	520 cm	75 cm	16 kg
C2	·650 cm	75 cm	20 kg
C7	1100 cm	85 cm	50 kg

All kinds of building materials are allowed through the sections and longitudinal lines of the hull must be convex. Steering rudders are allowed only in kayaks, though the maximum thickness of the rudderblade must not exceed 10 millimetres. No rudders are allowed in canoes and there are limitations on the amount of covering allowed. As well as weighing and measuring boats before a race, the first four are usually checked again afterwards!

The events contested in the sprints are:

World and Continental Championships

Men

500 m	K1	K2	K4	C1	C2
1000 m	K1	K2	K4	C1	C2
10,000 m	K1	K2	K4	C1	C2

Women

500 m	K1	K2	K4

Olympics

Men

500 m	K1	K2		C1	C2
1000 m	K1	K2	K4	C1	C2

Women

500 m	K1	K2

Courses should be still, windless water 2 metres deep. Special basins are used at World and Olympic championship level, so there are no currents, making each lane as fair as possible for each competitor. These basins are very sophisticated nowadays with electronic timing, special headphones for the officials who hold the sterns of the boats etc. The nine lanes, each 9 metres wide, are marked by a series of buoys. The starter gets races under way by shouting 'Ready', then 'Go!', or by firing a shot. If a competitor's paddle breaks within 15 metres of the start, a red flag is waved and the racers are recalled. Any entry that makes more than two false starts is disqualified.

Races over 500 and 1000 metres are over a straight course, but the 10,000 metre is run anti-clockwise up and down the water, though for the final 1000 metres the paddlers have to get in lane, the leader taking Lane 1, the second Lane 2 and so on.

67 International 2000 metre course at Holme Pierrepont National Water Sports Centre and Country Park (*courtesy of the Sports Council and the Nottinghamshire County Council*).

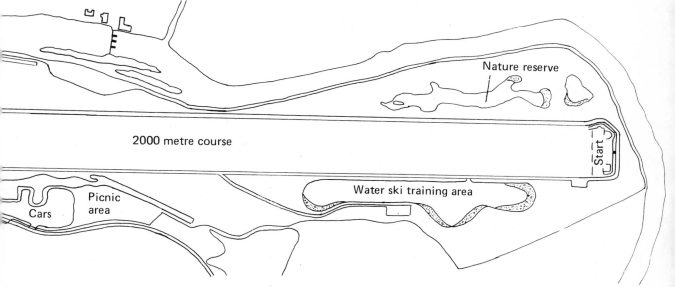

68 International regatta course, Sofia, Bulgaria.

While the tactic of 'wash-hanging' or 'wash-riding' is legal in the first 9000 metres of the 10,000 metre, it is forbidden in the two shorter races. Wash-hanging is a technique of using a rival's lead to advantage by sitting on the front edge of his wake, and thus having slightly less work to do as you get dragged along.

The 500 and 1000 metre events are not dissimilar. While the shorter distance tends to suit a powerful, stronger man or woman, the longer distance tends to suit an all-round fitter paddler. Although races are supposed to take place on courses where there is no advantage or disadvantage between racing in one lane or another, it is impossible to block off the wind, so that there will always be differences on many courses in conditions between the centre lanes and the side ones. Races at international level tend to have nine competitors and a spectator will always get an idea of wind conditions from the positioning of the paddlers in their 9-metre wide lanes. Rather than stick to the middle, they might cling to one side or the other to gain an advantage. The paddler himself can judge the wind from the waves blowing down or across the course. He also realizes that the wind strength at water level is often different 3 feet above the water.

Just before the start, the paddler is watching the bow of every other boat in the race. He is also half-watching the starter out of the corner of his eye, concentrating on everything he is saying. 'Up 2' or 'down 4' are his instructions to the boats in particular lanes, telling them to line up properly. In order to understand the starter, good paddlers always listen to the start of an earlier race to gauge both the tempo of his starting commands and his strictness.

They want to know how long he takes to say 'Ready . . . go!' and whether he is firm enough to call the competitors back if there is a slight false start. Many starters are regarded as 'soft' and will let experienced men jump ahead as soon as he says the first 'R' of 'Ready' . . . let alone 'go!' It is for this reason that a paddler watches his opponents. As soon as one moves, he knows he has to go too . . . and he knows he should be safe because it is the opponent who has jumped the gun. In fact, a paddler is allowed to have two false starts before he is disqualified, so that it is important to know how lenient the starter is.

The paddler should always ensure that he is not back-paddling as the starter gives his orders. His paddle must be in position, something that should be practised in training. If there are waves, he must learn to sit with one blade dipped in the water as a balance. Otherwise the blade must hover over the water ready to dig hard in.

This is a difficult manoeuvre in the single canoe or kayak — but even harder in the pairs or fours and teamwork is vital . . . unless everyone wants to go for a swim! Incidentally, if a blade breaks in the first few metres of a race, the paddler is entitled to race again, so a spare paddle should always be handy on the shore.

Under normal conditions, the paddler gives two good digs of the paddle to get the craft moving. The next four or five are to build up momentum before settling into a rhythm. However, if there is a head-wind, at the start, the paddler puts in less of these powerful strokes at the beginning. He will find that his stroking rate will be lower, as the boat is not travelling as fast. To help fight the wind, he needs more solid, powerful strokes and may even dispense with the first two hard strokes. By using steady strokes and lengthening them out sooner, he will retain his balance and find his rhythm sooner.

A side wind is the most difficult to deal with at the start since the craft rocks sideways as well as up and down, so keeping the tip of the paddle in the water is even more important; even if less power is generated, the stability is there. If the wind is blowing from behind the paddler, he can 'rev up' his pace without lengthening his stroke. Moving much faster, the stroke rate can increase by some five strokes per minute throughout the race. As the paddle and the paddler are both acting as a sail, he should sit upright and make the most of it!

The first 200 metres of the race requires maximum effort, both to get up speed and then to maintain it. Although the first two strokes are aggressive and the paddler has no time to breathe in and out regularly, he has to get into the rhythm that combines regular inhaling and exhaling in time with the paddle strokes. Once the 200 metre mark is reached, paddlers can level out the pace before going flat out again for the last 100-150 of the 500 metre or the final 200 of the 1000 metre.

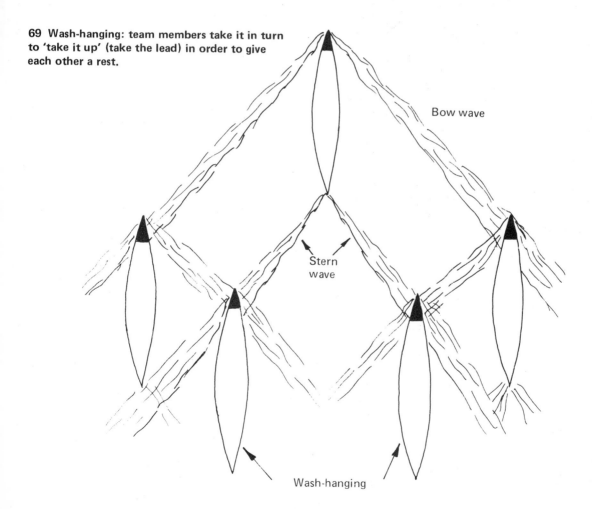

69 Wash-hanging: team members take it in turn to 'take it up' (take the lead) in order to give each other a rest.

Bow wave

Stern wave

Wash-hanging

Towards the end, the paddler again tries to 'rev up' whilst sustaining the effort put into each stroke. The effect of speeding up also helps to boost the enthusiasm. The pace for a K1 500 metre tends to be about 95 strokes per minute. At the start, the paddler would go out at 120 but could not maintain that for long, soon dropping to 110 before levelling out at 95. The pace would slip back up to 110 for the finish.

Although courses vary from competition to competition, the 10,000 metre at international level tends to consist of three laps of an oval course. The start is not in lanes like the shorter events but in a mass, with competitors lining up in numerical order as the result of a draw. However, the final 1000 metres *is* conducted in lanes. So the first man to reach the 9000 metre mark goes into Lane 1, the second man into Lane 2 and so on. The tenth man goes into Lane 1 and so on.

The idea behind this is to prevent a paddler using his opponent's wash. The technique of wash-hanging is not only allowed in the rest of the race but is the one single most effective tactic used. (It is forbidden in the 500 and 1000 metres, but is used in marathon racing.) In effect, the bow dips slightly and the stern is raised, so that the craft is virtually running downhill! The fractional assistance this gives is invaluable over 10,000 metres. Although the bow is submerged slightly, increasing the frictional resistance, the fact

71 Start of a ladies' sprint racing K1 competition (*Graham Ingram-Monk*).

that it is running downhill more than compensates, pulling the paddler along.

The only time that a paddler will find wash-hanging a disadvantage is travelling through big waves where the wash-hanger runs a greater risk of being swamped than does the lead boat. In order to get off the wash, the paddler pulls forward a little, and then, as soon as the wash has gone, drops back.

Tactically, there is a time to lead and a time to sit on the wash. Also, there are paddlers who prefer to do one or the other. Usually, there tends to be an arrow-head formation running down the course, with one man doing all the work, and everyone else trying to get as much rest as possible. In order to get maximum benefit from wash-hanging, the paddler needs to practise, as the faster a boat goes the further behind the wash he will drop. There are, in fact, two places to wash-hang. The first is at the side of the leader, off the bow wave, while the second is right behind the leader on the stern wave, though this is not as good. This is because the paddler often finds himself putting his paddle into a 'hole' left in the water by the leader's paddle. The turbulence this creates is both unnerving and unsteadying. On the other hand, if he is coming up behind a group, trying to jump from his group to the next, then this is the place he would tend to go, before making a break for the bow-wave at the side.

Unlike other sports where competitors mass

70 C1 sprint racing (*Graham Ingram-Monk*).

72 A K4 team at Holme Pierrepont
(*Graham Ingram-Monk*).

73 The Nottingham C7 crew at Fladbury
(*Graham Ingram-Monk*).

74 Norwegian K4 team at the 1972 Munich Olympics (*G. Mackereth*).

together (like cycling), there is little to be gained from tucking in *behind* an opponent. It is better to wash-hang irrespective of the wind direction, although in strong wind the competitor should stay on the leeward side in order to avoid being covered in spray flying off his opponent's paddles. 'Dirty' paddlers are a nuisance, especially for the paddler who elects not to wear a spraydeck. This extra water adds extra weight.

As courses are always covered in an anti-clockwise direction, the most important part of the race is the turn. When the paddler comes up to the marker buoy it is best to be in the lead. If he is on the inside of the leader, he may be forced into the smaller buoys that mark the edge of the course, and get caught up in the underwater ropes that hold them in place!

The leader does not or should not deliberately force opponents in this way. What he wants is the inside position on the turn as it is the shortest distance to paddle. At the same time, he can force his rivals off his wash. In order to get into this advantageous position, paddlers tend to 'burn' or sprint into the turns, positioning themselves to strike near

the front of the group. If a paddler cannot take the lead himself, he should tail the man who does round the bend, ready to get on his wash as soon as possible.

The leader can cause opponents a few headaches not only by getting the leading position but also by going away from the buoy as he goes round it in order to take the opposition wide.

By leaning the boat on its side, and kicking the tiller bar hard over (in fact, the tiller should always be slightly offset for 10,000-metre racing in order to get more leverage on to the rudder going into the bend), he can cut the corner while the opposition swing wide.

Another sprint at this point can take the leader of the pack clear, which means that they will have to work very hard in order to get back on to his wash.

Meanwhile, behind the leading group there will be several other groups of paddlers because the 10,000 metre tends to be run in groups. No matter what the group, a paddler must always follow anyone who makes a break. At the same time he must be aware of the make-up of groups because club members or good friends may have worked out tactical plans. One of these might sprint off, drawing opponents away at a tangent, while his club-mates sit back until the group has gone before making a break for the inside. The competitor who led everyone astray can then stop paddling while the rest of the field tries to make up the lost ground.

Unlike the 500 or 1000 metres, which are short enough to be paddles at or near maximum capacity, pacing is difficult in the 10,000 metre. If the paddler is content to aim for fourth or fifth place, then he can let the leaders dictate the pace, allowing them to outfox each other. Paddlers have good and bad patches during a race, often called second or third 'winds' so the pace can vary throughout. The hardest part is usually the first 1000 metres as competitors sort out which group they are going to race in, or make sure that no one else joins the leading group. Once that is settled, the next two laps are a little easier; everyone burns for the bends and straight paddles in between, with little or no jockeying for position.

Coming up to the last lap, there is far more burning going on between the bends, as paddlers try to drop their rivals, and to get away on their own in order to control the race. The strong survive this test of nerves and determination; the weak drop back.

Although generally the fittest man wins, it is not always so. There are lots of tactics, often rather unsavoury tactics, involved. These are, however, accepted as part of the robust fun of this event. For example, it is difficult to judge if a paddler means to cut across a rival's bow forcing him into the buoys, or whether he is tired and has made a simple mistake . . . ! Tempers do fray and 10,000-metre races can be quite physical, with paddles used more like weapons than means of propulsion!

Slalom

To many canoeists, the slalom is the most exciting event both for the spectator and the participant. The idea came from skiing where competitors show off their ability to twist and turn as they come down a mountainside, weaving in and out of 'gates', pairs of poles stuck in the snow. As canoeing and kayaking developed in Austria and Germany, it was winter-sports fans who transferred the idea of the slalom to fast-flowing mountain streams, which are Grade IV or V at international level.

Instead of sticking poles in the ground, they are suspended from wires above the water, and whereas the skier is not penalized for touching the gates, the canoeist and kayaker are. The water sport has the added complexity of asking competitors to take some gates going upstream or even reversing through other gates, and has team events where three paddlers set off to complete a course in the fastest time from

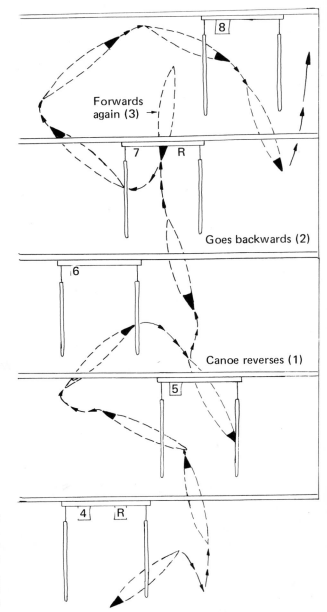

Typical slalom gate arrangement

75 Slalom course.

the first boat crossing the start line to the last one crossing the finish line. All events are decided on the faster of two runs by each entry.

Gate judges watch competitors, who start at one minute intervals, to see if they negotiate the course properly. Examples of penalties are touching a pole which collects 10 points, touching two poles 20 points, while pushing a gate, doing an Eskimo roll through a gate, negotiating a gate incorrectly or leaving out a gate altogether is worth a 50-point penalty. The gates themselves are clearly marked by numbers.

Times are converted to seconds, penalty points added on and the lowest score wins.

The slalom requires less space than the wild water, concentrating all the action into three or four minutes on a turbulent 700 to 800 metre stretch of water which helps generate interest and excitement. The first-time spectator sees that each gate is clearly marked with a number (up to 30 gates are set out) and at least four of them with an 'R' to indicate that it should be taken in reverse. The back of a gate also has numbers but these have a diagonal line through them to show that they should not be entered from that side.

Red and white striped poles must always be kept to the left of the competitor, with green and white poles to the right. In this way, the paddler knows at a glance where he is supposed to go as he takes the gates in strict numerical order. The course that is set must not only be suitable for both left- and right-handed paddlers but also for kayak and canoe specialists.

In countries where there is insufficient water to guarantee good slaloming conditions all the year round, artificial courses have been designed. Some are called 'weir slaloms', as they are run in the bubbling water below a weir. These are good for beginners as there are few rocks in the water. The 'controlled flow' slalom depends on water, often from a dam higher upstream, being released at a constant speed and volume in order to produce fair conditions for all competitors throughout a competition. The third type of course is totally artificial and costs millions of pounds to build.

There is a mixed event in the slalom. The classes with their specifications are as follows:

	Min. length	Min. width
K1	400 cm	60 cm
C1	400 cm	70 cm
C2	458 cm	80 cm

All kinds of building materials are allowed but the boats must be unsinkable (i.e. they must still float when filled with water) and have 'a loop of rope that will admit a hand, toggles or a line running the length of the boat from stem to stern.' No rudders are allowed but safety jackets and crash helmets must be worn and a spare paddle can be carried.

The categories at World and Continental Championships are:

Men
K1, C1, C2

Women
K1

Mixed
C2

Teams
3 x K1
3 x C1
3 x C2
3 x K1
3 x C2

The only time that slalom was a part of the Olympic Games programme was in 1972 when a special course was built at Augsburg with spectator accommodation. Although it provided tremendous sport, the cost of the operation made nonsense of the idea of 'sport for all'. It is perfectly feasible for Olympic, World and Continental Championships to be held on natural courses.

The boat itself has become highly sophisticated, rather like snow skis. It is in fact almost part of the competitor, very light in weight and designed to turn easily through all the gates. Its nose and tail are flattened so that it can be squeezed or sneaked under the poles which hang 10 centimetres above the water. This is a highly sensitive craft and can be used only for this event as it would be uncontrollable in a marathon or even a wild water event. The design enables the paddler to bend the rules to his advantage. Instead of having to paddle all the way through a gate, he gets his body through and then spins the boat underneath the pole so that he can turn and make a break out for the next gate down the course.

In terms of water technique and paddling, there is no substitute for gate practice. The paddler must be able to paddle forwards, backwards and sideways at gates, attacking them from all angles and in any sequence, able to put the paddles and the boat around and under the poles without touching them. His skills have to be as sharp on his left side as his right — it is no good being able to break out on one side and not the other, since courses are built to test both the natural left- and right-handers. Without

76 A paddler looks anxiously to see that he's kept within the slalom gates during the Llangollen town slalom (*Graham Ingram-Monk*).

this technical ability, no matter how fit the paddler is, he will never be able to put his strength and stamina to good effect on a slalom course. In the early part of the season, an hour's practice should be spent daily churning in and out of the gates, non-stop. After a few weeks, technique improves and it is important to try out three or four different courses during a session doing what paddlers call 'intervals'. These are consecutive runs over a course with less and less rest between runs as the paddler gets fitter and more efficient. All runs should be timed to keep the paddler up to the mark and it is important to keep varying the course so that he does not get used to one particular sequence of gates. Variations should be tried, with the paddler doing a break-out from a different side, doing a stagger gate or putting a gate in a different place. As usual, it is often important

to watch other more experienced paddlers to see how they train and perfect their techniques.

When trying new techniques such as changing the number of strokes between a break-out, it is not always necessary to do the gate at racing speed. It can be taken slowly to begin with, so that the strokes come in the right order with the correct amount of power. The paddler can introduce more speed once he has sorted out his technique.

In order to execute all the moves properly the paddler must be able to make his craft respond immediately. Sitting low in the boat with his hips, thighs and feet held firmly in place, he then knows that he can get instant response to any and every paddle stroke, even when he is upside down doing an Eskimo roll. A tight fit is ensured by extending the curved bucket seat of a kayak up to the cockpit coaming with hip-boards and by fitting the rim with extended thigh grips, and a fixed foot rest against which to push his knees, thighs and hips. The Canadian canoeist often uses a saddle-like structure to give extra support while kneeling down.

The amount of time to practise on a course before an event varies. Every paddler should get at least one trial run to see how the water flows and where the gates are placed. As the team event is often run before the individual event, this gives a paddler another chance to assess the course. Incidentally, gates marked with a T are team gates and all three crews have to get through this within 15 seconds if they want to avoid a penalty. Team events are not taken as seriously as individual events, so are often used as another means of reconnoitring the course. The paddler has to commit the course to memory, watching other entrants and observing the water from the bank. Some paddlers can be seen dropping twigs or match-sticks into the river to assess the currents. There is usually a slow, safe way down a course as well as a faster, riskier one. The individual has to decide which to take. There is a time to go flat out and a time to go slowly in order to negotiate a gate properly. A paddler can pick up time after the gate by using a fast turn, because slalom is a 'stop, start' event where acceleration is more important than rhythmical, graceful effort.

Too many paddlers give up mentally once they receive a penalty. They do not realize that almost everyone gets a penalty, especially on difficult courses. A race might be won by someone who incurs a couple of penalties, because it is the com-

77 International paddlers taking part in the men's team event, Llangollen town slalom. From left to right: Albert Kerr, Nicy Wain, Alan Hedge (*G. Mackereth*).

78 Ladies' World Champion, Kathy Hearn of the USA, in action at Jonquiere, Canada, 1979 (*G. Mackereth*).

bination of time and penalties that wins. A well-executed break-out will gain a couple of seconds over more cautious rivals who hope to make up time with a hard sprint between gates. At international level no time is wasted looking for the gates, as competitors memorize the whole of the course, never looking at the numbers.

It is often accomplished slalomists who are tempted to go on adventurous river expeditions where their split-second skill is used to negotiate treacherous water. The trip down Mount Everest in the Himalayas, the descent of the Colorado River through the Grand Canyon and the headwaters of the Blue Nile were all made by slalom men. Their ability to read water at speed made the journeys feasible.

It is worth remembering that any stroke that is used to keep the boat from capsizing, re-aligning it or making any other corrective move, is wasting time. The competitor must always be thinking ahead, like the chess player, so that he not only judges the angle at which he enters a gate but also the line

that has to be taken afterwards.

The design of the Canadian slalom boat has become more and more like the kayak in recent years, so techniques have become similar too. Often the most spectacular crews are the C2s, with their off-set cockpits. The teamwork needed with the single-bladed paddle is easy to understand when watching. Crew members often switch sides to get every possible advantage in a race, heaving away at the water using every combination of stroke to man-oeuvre through and under the gates.

Wild water

The events in canoeing and kayaking have often been compared with the same disciplines in skiing. The long-distance marathon races are like cross-country skiing, the wild water compares with down-hill, while slalom is a direct imitator of skiing's tightly turning slalom course.

Where marathon racing tests a competitor's endurance, wild water tests his strength, and slalom finds out his skill. This is, of course, a simplification, but in broad terms it is true.

Wild water has attracted paddlers for centuries.

There must have been some dare devils who shot rapids in their fragile craft centuries before the more aerodynamically shaped kayaks and canoes of today came on the scene. Even then, it was the canvas folding boat of the 1920s that attracted winter-sports fans to Germany and Austria on to the rocky snow-fed streams of the Alps.

In 1921, the first race took place on the River Isar, using folding boats. Soon Austria, Switzerland and Germany were holding international races to test the ability of their paddlers.

By 1934, the sport was widespread enough for a classification to be introduced, grading the rivers. The idea was to give paddlers a guide to unfamiliar streams. Then, as now, paddlers were reminded that those gradings were only a guide, not a dependable record. A rain storm, an hour of hot sun, the seasons — all can alter the character of a river from year to year, day to day and even hour to hour. In Europe, the table reads as follows:

Grade I Easy. Small infrequent rapids with easily definable course. Small regular waves. No problems of navigation through rapids and other obstructions.
Grade II Moderately difficult. Frequent rapids with regular waves, bends and eddies. Between

79 The American C2 crew shooting the top fall during the 1980 Europa Cup final at Seo D'Urquell, Spain (*G. Mackereth*).

rapids there are stretches of easy water. There will be light-to-moderately difficult stoppers.
Grade III Difficult. Passage through rapids requires manoeuvres to keep to the main course and to avoid whirlpools, strong eddies and waves, small falls and holes. Passage not easily seen from the river. Only short passages of light water between rapids. Holding stoppers.
Grade IV Very difficult. Long stretches of heavy rapid with high irregular waves, larger falls, strong current, powerful whirlpool, sharp curves and strong eddies. The way through the rapids is not easily recognized from the water and will often require inspection from the bank. Difficult holding stoppers.
Grade V Extremely difficult. Long, extremely difficult rapids with large, irregular and conflicting wave patterns. Extremely difficult falls, whirlpools, curves and eddies require precision paddling to keep to the correct course. The route though will not normally be recognizable from above and inspection of each rapid or section of rapid will be required.

**80 International C2 teams at the start of the
10,000 metre event, Nottingham International
regatta** (*Graham Ingram-Monk*).

Extremely powerful currents with a steep gradient.
Powerful and dangerous holding stoppers..
Grade VI Limit of navigability. There is a real risk
to life. Normally, river graded VI can be attempted
only at certain times of the year when water conditions are favourable.

The idea of such competition, held on a stretch of
white water about 3 kilometres long is to 'demonstrate a competitor's mastery of his boat in fast
moving white water while running a prescribed
stretch of water, choosing one's own route, in the
shortest possible time.'

The sport grew slowly, but exploded around 1960
when the fragile canvas kayak was virtually replaced
by the tougher and cheaper plastic boat. The whole
grading system became outdated almost overnight
as paddlers found that they could take on grades
that they would never have dreamed of (or had
nightmares about!) attempting before.

The Grade V or VI river of the past was considered
a severe danger to life and limb. Now it is extremely
difficult but possible to negotiate by the top-
class paddler. Not that a paddler should ever be
over-confident. That attitude of mind has been
more responsible for accidents than anything else.
Initially for the novice, a white water course should
just be enjoyed. Competition comes when the
paddler is totally at ease on a run, able to play in
eddies, practising forward ferry glides and shooting
rapids properly. In this way, he can find out the
tricks of the water by learning from the inevitable
mistakes. Slap support strokes and Eskimo rolls

become automatic and part of the paddler's sixth sense that produces the right stroke for the right situation without the fatal pause for thought.

One school suggests that paddlers (in appropriate conditions and equipment) float down the river in order to 'feel' the currents and eddies which the river produces. This idea is also useful for capsize situations, so that the novice does not find himself in swirling water for the first time under emergency conditions.

There is no substitute for practice, and there is no quicker way of learning a lesson than by observing other, better paddlers in action. Attending a club meeting, the paddler can soon tell who does best and how he is doing it. The more experienced man or woman will pick a way through the obstacles, looking for the V of the water, using the current as much as possible.

Apart from paddling down the course, the paddler can learn a lot just by looking at it from the bank. To help his memory he should draw a map or chart of the river marking the obstacles. He can also pace out the bank in order to get some idea of distance between the awkward parts of the river. A map can be used as a reference for the next visit . . . though water conditions should still be noted on the day.

Since the river changes according to the level of water, what may be a fast line in the spring may not be so fast in the summer or during a dry spell.

As courses vary according to the amount of water in them, so too does the structure of the courses themselves. When the water is low, organizers often use a bulldozer to move rocks around the river bed to present a new challenge or eliminate a really dangerous section.

When it comes to competitions it may be worth talking to other, experienced paddlers about the fast and slow lines of the course but their advice should be taken with a pinch of salt. After all, why should they give away the advantage of their experience to a new, young rival!

The course must be Grade III difficulty or greater. Courses less difficult are termed 'river races'.

The classes and their specifications are:

	Max. length	Max. width
K1	450 cm	60 cm
C1	430 cm	70 cm
C2	500 cm	80 cm

Again, rudders are prohibited on all boats.

The categories raced are:

Men
K1, C1, C2

Women
K1

Mixed
C2

Team events consist of three competitors in each category.

Timings are all-important as the fastest wins, in both individual and team events. There is only one timed run and as boats start off at regular 30-second or 1-minute intervals, there is a chance of overtaking. A competitor who is about to overtake shouts 'Free' and should be allowed past. At the same time, a competitor *must* always go to the aid of a fellow competitor who is in real danger. Safety equipment is the same as for slalom.

In assessing a fast line, the paddler may decide to go over a rock and risk slowing himself down, if that is a short cut around a corner. Or it may be faster to take a longer route if it is through good deep water. On the deep water stretches between rapids the paddler should lengthen his stroke, get his breathing right and get into a rhythm so the boat moves smoothly. When going down a rapid the paddler should keep off the peaks of the waves, staying to the sides of them where it is easier to maintain paddling rhythm. Stoppers should be avoided by finding gaps between them. Despite being knocked back by waves or losing momentum after going over a rock, the paddler must continue to attack the rapids. More time is lost there than anywhere else on the course.

If the paddler hits shallows in flat water where the water does not accelerate, he should increase his paddling rate. This sprinting lifts the bow up on to a plane where it will be easier to maintain speed.

Whether it is a kayak or canoe, the design characteristics of a white water boat are the same. Because a course has to be covered in the fastest time possible, the craft is longer than the slalom boat, with little rocker and a V-shaped hull to help speed it on its way down the river.

Although the basic paddle strokes apply in white water, there have been some new ones introduced that are used in competition, because they help to turn the boat quickly when it is travelling at speed. The most notable innovator was a Czech refugee who went to live in Switzerland. His name was Milos Duffek and he applied canoe paddling techniques

to kayaking. The C1 had a more developed technique because of the old-ruling that made it illegal to switch sides when paddling. Nowadays, either side is used, but Duffek, a former C1 champion, first demonstrated his technique at the 1953 World Slalom Championships at Merano in Italy. It evolved from the draw stroke often used in canoes, and Duffek leaned on his paddle to a degree no one had ever contemplated before. Duffek capitalized on the speed of the boat, the centrifugal force created and the change of the shape of the boat on the water as it leaned. His strokes perhaps have slightly less effect now because boats with their modern flat-decked appearance produce less benefit from turning on their sides. Duffek turns are made without a loss of forward or reverse speed which helps to save the vital fractions of a second in competition. However, it is impossible to attempt a Duffek without a thorough knowledge of the basic strokes. They require the whole-hearted weight and commitment of the paddler on to his paddle because the brace is no longer a redressing manoeuvre applied to the side in tossing waves, but rather a forward-oriented

81 British international Iain Freestone in wild water (*Colorsport*).

pivot used at speed.

To do the Duffek turn properly into an eddy, the paddler accelerates the boat, holding his paddle as for a 90° side brace, but instead of inserting his paddle at the side, he move his lower arm forward, bends his upper arm still further and leans his torso forward. The paddle blade is inserted at a high climbing angle into the current, well off the bow. Hanging his weight on to the brace, he automatically begins to draw his bow round. When he is suspended with his paddle, the kayaker is like an ice-skater leaning into the edge of his skate with his stability far greater than when he is sitting upright — but that stability only lasts as long as he has momentum!

Learners often feel that the stroke is ineffective. More often than not, they are unsuccessful because they do not risk as much as they should when leaning on the paddle. In such a position, the paddler may think that his full weight is on the paddle but very often this is not the case. It is important that the paddle is planted far enough forward, because if it is allowed to go to the stern, the boat will turn the opposite way. It is good to practise different positions of both the upper and lower arm. Often the upper arm seems to go behind the head, but this is to get the lower paddle blade further forward and also slightly closer in to the boat if necessary. On flatter water this becomes more important than having to lean out but is very good practice to get the confidence of an exaggerated lean for white water paddling. The angle at which the paddle is in the water is very important, and this has to be adjusted to suit the underwater currents. Very often the current on the surface is not the same as the current that the paddler is pulling on, so he must rely on the feel of the paddle blade to judge the power and degree of the stroke. This can only be learned from experience.

Marathon

Marathon racing is also described as long distance racing or down river racing. Whatever it is called, it involves paddling further than the longest sprint event, the 10,000 metre, which is about 6 miles.

The events that come under the marathon heading are as varied as the estuaries, lakes and rivers of the world. Whereas sprint events take place in concrete basins or calm, still lakes, marathon races usually take place in natural conditions; having said that, man-made canals are also used. Different races cater for different classes of boat, and some are happy to mix the entries even to the extent of allowing both kayaks and canoes together.

The technique and equipment is much the same as for the 10,000 metre, but paddlers have to remember that the kayak rudder can be an encumbrance — dropped during a portage it would break. However, of course, the over-stern rudder would be used in conditions where there are obstacles since it would slip up. On marathon courses, rafts of reeds and grasping weeds are hazards that have to be taken into account in just the same way as the more obvious obstacles like weirs, dams and locks. These man-made obstructions demand the technique called 'portaging', carrying the boat to the next place of water. This short stage on land can decide who wins or loses a race.

Marathons begin with a mass start, though the top competitors (judged on previous results) are often seeded. The start can be on a strip of bank or beach, and if the event is seeded it ensures that the best competitors are at the front, ready to push off when the signal is given. Starting with pairs of fours

demands practice so that every member of the crew knows what his role is. This teamwork comes into play at the portages. Paddlers often burn (sprint) to get to the right place in order to leap out of the boat . . . but the question is . . . what is the right place?

Good runners might prefer to come to the bank at any easy landing place that is well before the lock or weir. The longer run suits them, where a less able runner may try to get nearer to the obstacle. Problems arise when a paddler arrives at his planned disembarkation point to find someone else blocking his path. If there is a narrow gap in the bank, the second paddler will just be wasting his time waiting to get ashore. This emphasizes the importance of reconnoitre before the race, which will not only reveal good places to land, but also alternative sites in case of emergency.

On the portages, it is the cross-country runner with plenty of endurance in his legs who does best. However, in a tandem the timing and understanding must be perfect. Stories abound concerning the bowman who picks up the front of the boat and moves off before his companion is ready. The result can be fatal, as a kayak drops, not on its stern, but on its rudder . . . which breaks off, eliminating the crew from the race immediately.

The majority of races are completed in an afternoon, or a day at the most. It is only the well-publicized 'classics' that incorporate overnight stops and special sprint legs. Often, a country will have a series of marathon races in which paddlers pick up points — like a Grand Prix motor-race — with the best team winning at the end of the season.

While travelling along, paddlers use special devices in order to refresh themselves. One is a plastic bottle that is slung round the neck, fixed to the foredeck, or behind the paddler, and has a long plastic tube fitted with a non-return valve so that the paddler can suck up liquid without stopping.

Marathon racing has great potential for development, because of the number of people who can take part and because of its spectator appeal. Many think that it is only a question of time before the trend towards professional racing which has grown in Canada and the United States will reach Europe, especially Britain and Austria. The appeal to spectators is the exciting mass start, the jockeying for position, the clashing of paddles over the opening 500 metres, and then being able to follow the race through the countryside. Some of the major races attract huge entries. For the Devizes-Westminster Race in England there are regularly 250 entries, for

82 Tackling the Avon descent
(*Graham Ingram-Monk*).

the Gudena Marathon in Denmark there can be as many as 1000 while in the United States as many as 2500 crews turn out for major races.

Marathon paddling is relatively new, so the rules are constantly under review. The various countries have different rules and different traditions. In Europe K1s and K2s are the most popular boats, while the C2s are the craft that Americans and Canadians prefer. While the Europeans consider ten miles to be a marathon, North Americans think that 25 miles is average.

For several years, devotees of marathon racing have been pushing for acceptance of their favourite form of canoeing at international level. The ICF (International Canoe Federation) finally recognized marathon as a competitive discipline in its own right at its 1980 Congress at the Moscow Olympic Games. A Sub-Committee was set up to standardize the rules and regulations for continental and world championships. A Grand Prix system already exists whereby points are won in each of a series of races. The competitor with the most points at the end of the series wins the title. However, it is anticipated that a world championship would be decided as the result of a single race. The Sub-Committee has to decide how to appease the schools of thought on marathon racing — one group prefers deep water racing, the other insists on having stretches of white water.

However, the variety of courses used in marathon or long distance as it is sometimes called, is as varied as nature itself. Some include wild water, some shallow as well as deep water, others have only deep water. Most include portages. While the ideal of standardizing courses is commendable, it is to be hoped that the essential character of well-established races is not changed (see section on classic races, p.115). Like cross-country racing in athletics, all courses are different, yet none should give any one athlete an advantage over fellow competitors.

Top-class paddlers in Europe use Olympic-type sprint kayaks for marathon racing. In deep water conditions, the normal rudder works well, but in shallow-water events an 'over-stern' rudder is used.

83 Paddlers in action during the K1 marathon on the river Wey (*Graham Ingram-Monk*).

Made of aluminium, this is designed to lift up when it hits an underwater obstacle. As it is not as firm as an 'under-stern' rudder, it is less effective when it comes to 'wash-hanging', the technique already described. Canoes have no rudders.

As for equipment, a spray-cover, zipped or unzipped, depending on personal preference, is important in kayak events. Paddles tend to be slightly longer than sprint paddles, though this again is governed by personal preference. In North America, the 'bent' paddle is popular. It has a deliberate kink in it which encourages a very fast paddling action, quite different from a sprint style. The paddle itself is quite legal as ICF rules merely define canoe racing as a discipline using single-bladed paddles.

In marathon racing, the paddler looks for rhythm rather than all-out effort, conserving energy as much as possible. While wash-hanging is a major feature of

84 Peter Healy paddling through the Red gum stands in the Barmah Forest near Echuca on the Murray River, Australia.

both the 10,000-metre sprint race and the marathon, the burn (sprint) is used differently. In the 10,000 metre paddlers always burn as they go into the turns. In marathon, the burn is used sparingly but effectively. With a number of obstacles to be negotiated, paddlers usually burn as they come up to a portage in order to get a head start when they have to get out of their boats and run. If they are too hasty, paddlers can 'take a swim' as they try to gain time by getting back on to the water again. Portaging has to be practised time and time again.

Practice on the course itself is always an advantage, so that shallows, rocks and other obstacles can be analysed and a fast course plotted. Paddlers must always avoid shallows, keeping to the deep water. Weeds also slow down progress. If there is no chance to practise ahead of time, any advice from fellow competitors should always be taken with a pinch of salt, as gamesmanship is not unknown in canoeing!

Once a decision has been made on tactics, either

as a result of a trial run or a river guide, there must always be an alternative and flexible plan. After all, most obstacles are clear for all the paddlers to see, and they will all be burning at similar points or taking similar courses. If paddlers find that they are not in a position to dictate tactics, they have to be versatile enough to look for any alternatives.

Unlike many competitive events, marathons are run over natural courses, so at different times of year, different water conditions pertain. What is a shallow, ditch-crawling event one year can be rough and exciting the next. Marathon paddlers have to be prepared for any eventuality. Heavy overnight rain can demand the use of spray covers, buoyancy aids and crash helmets. The race organizer may insist that these are worn in all conditions. Whatever happens, paddlers should have all their equipment to hand, ready for any eventuality. It is always better to wear a buoyancy aid and crash helmet that is comfortable, rather than having to borrow one that may not fit properly. There is nothing more irritating than competing in gear that is too loose or too tight.

CHAPTER 8
The Role of the Coach in Competitions

The manager/coach

In the early days of his competitive career a committed paddler will tend to accept, in an almost unthinking or automatic way, the dictates of his manager/coach. But if the relationship between the two is to be properly developed and balanced, then the paddler will find he is making an increasingly important contribution to his training, as time progresses, when it comes to an evaluation planning.

In the pursuit of excellence, it is absolutely necessary that both coach and paddler realize the need for hard physical work, the acquiring of the right behavioural patterns, and the development of intellect and poise in the approach to competitions.

The part played by the paddler in the preparation of training schedules or yearly programmes is important. A British marathon paddler illustrated his role in the paddler/coach relationship by saying that, 'when preparing for a competition such as the Gudena Marathon, my own experience, from the previous year, can be brought to bear and my recall is of assistance to the coach in helping me direct myself, or in giving directions for a subsequent competitive event.'

The role of the manager/coach is immensely important in the psychological preparation of a paddler. That same paddler said he was 'always aware that my coach never spoke in a negative fashion before a competition — he always concentrated on being buoyant and on making positive predictions'. The coach's desire for a good performance, if given to the paddler in a well-timed, well-judged, pre-race chat, can have a stimulating and positive effect.

The coach indeed must continually motivate the paddler throughout the whole pre-race period. He does this by being confident and by being totally convincing in his expectations of success, as long as the psychological rehearsal, stretching and warm-up routines are strictly adhered to.

Tactics, the same as long-term strategies, are seldom plucked out of a hat on the day. They have to be planned and rehearsed throughout the whole of the preparatory training period. Occasionally, particularly in National, Olympic or World Championship team situations, a paddler may find himself placed under and working with a coach with whom he is not familiar. Then it is unwise for the nominated national coach to try to alter the approach of a paddler who has had success under his own personal coach. It is wiser, by far, for the national coach to structure his approach to fit in with the paddler's previous experience and training.

Realistic targets have to be set before an event. Undoubtedly these must be based on past performances in both competition and training and should in no way be arbitrary expectancies of the coach! Coaches should declare at least one level below expectancy.

Behaviour patterns, on the part of the paddler, to all competition, have to be stimulated and developed by the coach. The coach has to develop a consistent approach to his charges and must be detailed, to the extreme, in his own preparations and administration. Distractions, no matter how personal and domestic, should not be allowed to interfere by either coach or athlete. This has often proved difficult to achieve in many easy-going Western societies but is nevertheless essential. Come the day, both the coach and the athlete (the 'team') should be aware of the challenge they face, how they are going to match up to it and, most importantly, that they are to have success. These are the important dictates in the establishment of a successful manager/coach-athlete relationship.

Certain attributes are common to all outstandingly good coaches: experience (which is often labelled 'common sense'), intelligence, commitment, dedication, enthusiasm, the capacity for infinite and detailed planning, and above all the ability to handle his charges or his guy. There is strong evidence that an outstanding coach can move from one sport to another, in which he has little previous experience and still be successful. Although he may have no technical experience of the sport, he will almost certainly have the physiological and psychological skills which are often transferable. Technical knowledge can be acquired in a comparatively short period of time, if the coach applies himself to the subject. In many sports coaches and managers only 'switch-on' to their sports once or twice a week — the successful ones live their sport and their responsibilities every spare moment.

Many countries fall short on success because few of their coaches, if any, are fully conversant in all three of these essential attributes.

The path to success is summarized by British coach and old colleague, Ron Emes, who says that:

It is necessary, by a process of personal discovery, to confirm the often-quoted though rarely believed claim within the world of sport, that there is no magical formula for improving performance, no secret methods, no instant success. There is only hard work, intelligent application and determination to succeed, based upon systems of training that have been well-tried and long established and which are available to all those who are willing to seek them out.

Competitions – before and after

It is very important to prepare for a competition, and it is equally important to reflect after a competition on what went right as well as what went wrong — in military terms 'briefing' and 'debriefing'. The coach has an important role to play in both of these.

With competitions traditionally at a weekend, say on a Saturday, a training schedule would follow this pattern. Monday's workout would be quite hard, because a competition, in terms of pure physical output, is never likely to be as hard as a training session for the top level athletes. Tuesday's session would also be normal, though an athlete would probably use a modified programme for Wednesday. Certainly, for a canoeist, contact with the water on Thursday and Friday is essential to maintain rhythm prior to the competition. This may mean just going out for a paddle.

Meals are important. A heavy meal the day before the competition is all right, but on the day itself competitors are likely to be on the water fairly early. Two breakfasts are suggested. A first consisting of bread or buns and cake with mashed bananas and some sugar, but not too much liquid. Later, after getting some fresh air, and limbering up and going for a paddle, a second breakfast should be eaten which is about the same as the first with possibly some ham and eggs. The competitor should not eat any more until after the main event is over. He has taken a lot of carbohydrate which in the process of three or four hours will be converted into sugar by his body. Warming up is dealt with in

the interview with Einar Rasmussen in the last chapter, in which he describes his routine. A series of stretching exercises described in the training section is also recommended.

The coach's responsibility

As far as possible before an event the coach should systematically go through all the preparatory routines and make sure that the paddler has everything he needs to get on the water. He has to take the pressures off the athlete. That includes checking on things such as starting positions and boat numbers. Are the paddles all right, is the boat all right, is the seat secure, is there a wing-nut to fasten the seat down? All of these things should be checked through quietly between the caoch and the paddler before the race. Nothing should be left until the last moment. Another valuable role a coach can fulfil is in helping the paddler to withdraw so as not to become over-excited or over-involved before the event. Not all athletes like this period of contemplation but many do, and the coach should be available if required. Having said that, at no stage should the athlete become so dependent upon a coach that he is totally incapable of functioning in a solo situation. In any case, once a canoeist is on the water he is on his own and no coach can help him. So a competitor should not falter, just because his coach isn't there.

Team members often like to cheer on a fellow member in a race. Although this is obviously encouraging, in the best disciplined teams (where there is a corporate identity and team members do support each other) competitors for the next two events will have been withdrawn by the manager/coach to begin their own preparations for their event. It does no good to go and cheer someone else on and then rush back to begin preparation for a race. Competitors have to forego watching the exciting events to prepare themselves for their own races.

Once again, it just comes down to preparation, thinking about all the things that have to be done and even anticipating all the things that should *not* happen. Check the start time. The 24-hour clock is not understood in all parts of the world. Sometimes local time or summer-time changes the clocks, and too often competitors arrive an hour early or an hour late for their events. Times need to be checked and double checked.

Even then things can go wrong. During the Gudena Marathon in Denmark when I was supporting two members of the British team, their equipment for the next stage of the race was in a car that I had hired. Unfortunately, the first paddler to arrive had got his equipment out — I myself having opened the car — but then he locked the car with all the keys inside. Now the British team were in a very critical position as they were leading at the time and favourites for the gold medal. Fortunately, I went back to lay out the second paddler's equipment and discovered the problem early enough to get help. A man mending the roads lent me a sledge-hammer but I couldn't break the car window. So I approached a policeman for help and eventually it took four blows from a crowbar before I was able to smash the rear window and get in. I was just in time as the second paddler was arriving. He got his stuff and was able to change and get on the water without any hassle. That was my responsibility. Had I not bothered to check, there would have been a calamity — as it was there was a bill for a broken window on return of the car!

At the same time, even the organizers are fallible. They might assume everybody knows the way from A to B, say from the hotel to the course. But people can be misled. Just because you see somebody with a canoe on top of his car it doesn't mean he is necessarily taking part in the regatta with you. I know of someone going to an event who was following a K1 which happened to be approaching the town where the race was taking place. He followed it right the way round the perimeter of the town and off onto a road going south. He was about 30 miles south of the venue before realizing the car he was following was going to the coast. He turned round and got back only just in time to get on the water!

So, always, always, allow sufficient time for things to go wrong.

After the competition

After an event, the competitor has to do two things. One is to warm down, which is a physical thing. The other is mental — the 'autopsy', the 'post-mortem', the 'debrief'. The body behaves just like a highly tuned machine, so it is not a good idea to race it flat out and then leave it with everything boiling over to cool down too rapidly. It has to be done slowly. So, after a race the sensible competitor will paddle on for a few minutes and slowly relax. Then he will get out, park his boat, shower, dry off, change and bring his body back to a normal state. It is wholly unwise to drop the boat on the bank and rush off in wet gear to start watching other races before having a shower and cool down.

Just as in the engine certain substances are a by-product of combustion, there are also 'exhaust' gases in the human body where combustion is taking place as the body burns fuel. There are by-products like carbon dioxide and lactic acid which the body needs to get rid of and the whole warming-down process is designed to do this.

The second thing after a race is the debrief. If the competitor has won, was it according to plan or was it unpredicted? Was it a win despite the plan? If he didn't win, did he lose because of one or two unforced errors? Or because the man who beat him was, on the day, that much better? If so, what has he got to do to put that right? All this is very important and should be done within hours of the event, not within a matter of days. It must be done while the race is still fresh in the mind of the paddler, his coach and his manager. There should be discussion but never recrimination.

It is worth remembering that most competitions are not just one race. There have often been qualifying rounds and semi-finals as well as finals, but no matter when the competition ends, the competitor should go out the next day and have a *hard* training session as part of the warming-down process. It is psychologically bad to think that because he has worked so hard in a competition he deserves a day off. The actual races may be tougher psychologically and mentally but that is all the more reason why the hard training session shoudl follow. The next day should be a rest day. Like climbing mountains, one has to go up slowly and down equally slowly.

In all training there has to be a measure of unpredictability, which is why it is useful to have a coach. The coach can build in something unexpected. He can say, 'OK, this is the programme,' and right out of the blue he can shout 'Do this!' — demanding an exercise that is not scheduled. This causes the athlete to adjust to the unforeseen, the unexpected. Nothing should be so routine and so rhythmical that the body or the mind cannot adjust quickly. This is particularly important when moving from one country to another; the athlete must be able to acclimatize and habituate himself easily. This can be made easier by varying the training so that the mind as well as the body is used to adapting quickly.

This is also useful during the competition itself. For example, when there is a false start, a paddler might get cautioned. He has to accept that and settle down to get ready for the second start. Quite often the competitor blamed for a false start has a fear of disqualification and will throw away the race. A good athlete should be able to accept the decision and adjust quickly. If the competition is cancelled for the day, the well-prepared athlete will be able to adapt his preparation schedule and again lift himself mentally and physically for the delayed race.

So the post-competition phase has to be taken just as seriously as the preparation and that again is just part of the coach-athlete relationship.

Here are some remarks by ex-Olympic paddler and canoe statesman, John Dudderidge:

The elite sportsman aspiring to achieve the summit of international competition, e.g. an Olympic title, must be prepared for total dedication over a period of years. This means keeping family responsibilities, girl friends and other recreation in proper perspective. The term at the top is short — the satisfaction is worth the sacrifice.

There is need for balanced development. The top athlete must use his intelligence — mental training is as important as physical.

The representative athlete will inevitably be looked upon as an unofficial ambassador and as such must project a worthy image through sportsmanship, dignity, courtesy and through an ability to express himself.

British athletes and many others in Western countries are continually bombarded by spurious distractions prevalent in society today.

The top echelons are now better supported financially than ever before.

There is now a need to take a leaf out of the book of our opponents and start early in schools and youth organizations. There is also a need for a greater scientific approach to the training of coaches and trainers at all levels for those taking responsibility for coaching the elite sportsman.

CHAPTER 9

Other Canoe Sports: Sea, Surf, Polo, Sailing and North American Canoeing

Sea canoeing

A man who is not afraid of the sea will soon be drowned,
For he will be going out on a day he shouldn't.
But we do be afraid of the sea,
And we do only be drowned now and again!

J.M. Synge

Originally, the kayak was a sea-going form of transport, but it is on inland water that it is mostly used now. Canoeing at sea is a very tricky matter, because there is little doubt that the sea is the most unpredictable and powerful element. The winds, tides, storms, fog and currents should make any canoeist think twice before trying his or her luck on the ocean. Then there are hazards such as big shipping, rocks and sandbars, all of which must be avoided. Sadly, many lives are lost each year by canoeists who think they have enough experience or have prepared properly for even a short journey.

This report from the London *Daily Telegraph* of an incident in 1980 shows just how dangerous a seemingly easy journey can be . . . .

A canoeist who floated for six hours in bitterly-cold seas after his 15ft boat capsized described yesterday how he felt on seeing the yacht which saved him: 'It was like winning the pools'.

Mr John Jones, 42-year-old tyre inspector and father of two, had to battle against unconsciousness as 'huge, vicious' waves swept him to what he believed would be certain death in the Bristol Channel.

He was rescued when the crew of the 22ft Tian Kwang spotted him in his bright yellow life-jacket, weakly waving his arms and blowing almost inaudibly on a whistle.

Before setting off on a 25-mile cycle ride yesterday, Mr Jones told of the ordeal he underwent on Saturday when conditions in the Channel suddenly changed from force two — officially a 'slight breeze' — to force six, with winds of up to 31 miles an hour.

He had been returning from Denny Island midway between Portishead, Somerset, and the Welsh coast, a three-mile voyage.

'Many people will say I was a bloody idiot to be out there at all,' he said at his home in Brookfield Park, Weston, Bath. 'But I'm a very experienced canoeist.

I checked the weather before leaving and it is accepted that you can canoe in force two without danger. When the weather changed it was something extraordinary.

I bowed for some time against the huge vicious waves, but was hit by two crashing together. All hell let loose and I found myself upside down. With all the equipment I had it wasn't possible to right myself properly.

I knew I would be finished if I came out of the canoe, but there was nothing I could do about it. Although I tried to swim I knew it was hopeless and could see the coastline disappearing slowly from sight.

Three or four times I was aware of losing consciousness. On one of those occasions I lost my grip on the canoe and paddle.'

Not being particularly religious he 'sort of said goodbye' to his wife Margaret, 41, fully believing he was about to die.

'Then I saw the yacht. That it should be there on that tack just as I was coming up on a wave was an almost impossible combination of circumstances.'

In the Tien [sic] Kwang were Mr Colin Burgin, his daughter, Philippa, 15, and a friend, Mr Mike Jessop.

A lucky escape! Remember that in low sea temperatures the ability to handle a canoe is not enough. As well as having good stamina, a sea canoeist has to be able to navigate, read the currents and tides, and should be able to interpret the weather conditions that can change so rapidly. Not surprisingly, those paddlers who specialize in sea canoeing seem to be a breed apart. They lavish days of care and attention on their craft, which are specially designed. Boats are usually about 15 feet long, and often the shapes and decorations used by the Eskimos of the Arctic are reproduced by enthusiasts who argue over the merits of the straight bow, curved bow or clipper bow. As the boat has to cut its way through waves, the curved bow is most popular as it tends to protect the paddler's face by deflecting the flying salt water.

A high foredeck helps to take the impact of rough water, while a low rear deck allows the water to

100

run away. The high foredeck also provides the paddler with a bit more leg room which is important on long voyages. After all, there is no inviting grassy bank to paddle to when the legs need stretching!

Buoyancy has to be excellent and bulkheads are often designed to act as separate water-tight compartments. The usual foam or plastic bags can be used but these cut down on the amount of important equipment that needs to be carried. It almost goes without saying that spray covers must be as water-tight as possible and that wetsuits should be worn in cool conditions. While ordinary paddles can be used, many sea canoeists prefer to use the longer, slimmer bladed paddles favoured by the Eskimos.

85 Pete Midwood completing the first single-handed crossing of the Irish Sea in 1978.

On the other hand, they often paint them bright orange with fluorescent paint to help an aerial rescue plane. The accent on rescue is always there in sea canoeing. Buoyancy aids or life jackets must always be worn, but then the list of more unusual equipment begins. Flares and smoke signals are carried ready to rocket into the sky in case of distress. Decklines (taut ropes) run around the deck and maps and a compass are protected from the wet and tied down in a well in the deck in front of the paddler. Paddle parks (metal clips) stand by ready to hold a paddle or spare paddle and a first aid kit and waterproof torch are kept below deck. Also hidden away there will be a pump so that any water from unexpected waves that get through the spray cover can be rapidly evacuated. As well as food, water and clothing, many sea canoeists carry further emergency equipment such as a signalling mirror, a parachute flare, a strobe beacon and radio equipment, not to mention a urine bag.

It must be obvious now that the sport is dangerous, even if some sea canoeists do tend to embellish the mystique that surrounds it. It can never be recommended for the lone paddler and never for the novice. Having stressed this, it is enjoyable and hundreds of canoeists around the world get hours of pleasure out at sea, or following the coastline.

Technique

Leaving or returning to shore is usually a matter of timing. A hard shove-off at the right moment and the canoe will float out on a wave; by catching an incoming wave, the paddler will arrive high up the beach. Strong wind or rough conditions will make launching or landing a wet, scrambled affair for even the most experienced participant.

Out at sea, the waves can come in any and all directions. If a wave hits a paddler sideways on (a beam sea) he can hold himself upright by using the paddle as a brace (the paddle brace). If the waves are from behind (a following sea), the technique is similar to surfing and is a distinct help, like a following wind for a runner. A head sea, on the other hand, can be quite tiring, even if it is not as dangerous as it looks. The lightness of the canoe means that it sticks to the surface of the water, the sharp bow punching through the crest of the wave and even hanging in mid-air for a second before slapping down on to the water again. A touch from the paddle will keep the boat balanced up. Yet again, sea canoeing requires experience . . . not only to obtain full enjoyment, but at times for survival.

Surf canoeing

The media in general, but television in particular, has high-lighted the sense of adventure and the sheer excitement to be obtained on a surf beach. The big stuff of television spectaculars and commercials is strictly for the paddlers with long experience.

Surf of the right kind for canoe surfing cannot be found everywhere in the world and, inevitably, the development of this exciting discipline of canoeing will be confined to the seaboards of certain countries.

Gently shelving sandy beaches and offshore winds are necessary to produce the right canoe-surfing conditions.

Surfers can opt, once proficient, for a number of variations on a theme. Firstly, there is the offshore area where the waves, before they have broken, provide a stimulating fast-moving ride. This area of the 'green waves' is for the experienced paddler. One up, again, is the breaking wave — again, not an area for the novice, which provides a superb vehicle for fast-moving feats and manoeuvres.

Finally the 'soup', the turbulent shallow area up the beach where the waves are no longer awesome and which provides an excellent 'nursery' area for the novice.

It is essentially necessary for the novice to take his first steps in small surf and waves and, preferably, under the personal supervision of an experienced surfer. Surfing is a natural progression from slalom and white-water paddling, many of the skills being transferable. As an activity it lends itself, both in terms of safety and enjoyment, as a group activity. The safety aspect is paramount and no one should surf on his own — minimum number for obvious reasons is a pair with only one in the water at any one time. The shore-based man, in a pair, and the designated rescuer in a party has got to be constantly aware of what is going on and is not around to occasionally assist in emptying water out of a kayak.

Before taking to the water the novice paddler must be aware of the particular characteristics of the beach being used — including the location of rocks, inlets, sand-banks or sand-bars. The nature of the sea-bed, its steepness and general characteristics, has a direct effect on the waves and their speed.

When taking to the water the paddler should never paddle out through surfers coming in on waves. He must make his way out, into deeper water, well clear of the area designated for surfing. On well-organized beaches special areas are set aside for surf canoeists and surf boarders but where these conditions do not exist then it is essential to keep well clear of swimmers. A canoe, even when not travelling at speed is dangerous; flat out it is positively lethal. If, for some reason, a collision seems imminent, then the paddler must deliberately capsize his kayak, thus allowing the wave he is riding to pass by. The upturned kayak, with the paddler's body in the water, will brake rapidly. The more competent canoeist will judge when the wave has completely passed him and executing an Eskimo roll will right himself.

If a paddler gets into trouble the rescue should

be left to one of the most experienced surf canoeists present. An inexperienced rescuer might well create a double incident and end up in need of rescue himself. In any rescue situation the first consideration is the paddler — the fate of the kayak is of secondary, if any, importance.

It is safest for only one person to surf each wave and, consequently, when a paddler sees a wave he wishes to surf he must make his intention quite clear by 'calling' for it. It is possible for two paddlers to start to surf the same wave and should this happen then the paddler with the less desirable position must 'drop-off-it'.

In the early stages of surfing the paddler will almost certainly find himself capsizing with regular monotony. This latter statement underlines the statement made elsewhere in this book that it is wise to learn to 'roll' early in a paddling career — it enhances enjoyment, attainment and safety; all of equal importance if a sport or recreational activity is to be rewarding, and surf very much can be. In terms of pure time then, the ability to Eskimo roll will save endless journeys to the beach in order to empty out the kayak.

Travelling across a wave will give a faster run than will travelling directly towards the beach. To steer the kayak and to stop it from broaching the waves a 'stern rudder' will be necessary. This manoeuvre is accomplished by putting one of the paddle blades, vertically to the surface, into the water towards the rear of the kayak. The blade must also be on the 'down-wave' side of the craft. If the paddle blade is put into the water on the 'up-wave' side then this will encourage the craft to broach even more and, possibly, turn it back through the

86 Using stern rudder.

wave. If to 'break-out' over the top of the wave is the manoeuvre the paddler wishes to achieve then the putting in of the paddle in the telemark position on the 'up-side' of the kayak will bring about the desired response.

Anticipating the wave is important and can only be learned by considerable and diligent practice. The paddler should wait until the wave begins to pick up the stern of the boat and then two or three quick paddle strokes will start the kayak running down the wave. The paddler may, at first, time this badly and find himself missing the selected wave. The experienced surfer will instinctively know when he has had the best use of a wave and will turn out of it using a telemark turn manoeuvre and will then paddle back out to sea.

If a paddler finds he is broaching and moving broadside to a wave, and in the early stages he will, he must remember not to lean away from the wave or he will find himself capsizing. By leaning into the wave and placing the paddle blade, horizontally, on top of the wave he will find the wave supports him and will push him sideways to the beach.

The more complex and advanced manoeuvres of 'looping' and 'pop-out' can follow on from this basic skill. The novice may even find himself doing a 'pop-out' unwittingly. A 'pop-out' is when the bow of the kayak buries itself into the water or sand and the wave pushes the canoe into the vertical position. It is important that the paddler leans hard back along the rear deck of the kayak during this manoeuvre.

Surf canoeing is undoubtedly exciting but sheer force and the nature of big waves, and the speeds attained, make it all the more imperative that correct well-made equipment is used. Second-rate kayaks, for example, would not stand up to the constant

87 Popping out.

buffeting for very long. The joins of the kayak must be very strong and sound to withstand the enormous stresses which they will experience, whilst the seat and cockpit rim need to be firmly fixed and secure. The foot-rest can be either of a 'fixed' or 'fail-safe' type but, again, whatever type it is, it must be very strong and constructed to standards that enable it to withstand great force. If a foot rest were to break there would be the strong possibility of the paddler slipping off the seat and down inside the kayak — becoming firmly and inextricably wedged in it!

Buoyancy within the kayak is important in all aspects of canoeing and surf canoeing is no exception. As much buoyancy material as possible should be wedged in the stern and bow of the craft filling the spaces behind and in front of the cockpit. If the space in front of the foot rest is well filled it becomes an added safety precaution as it would assist in preventing the paddler sliding down inside his craft. Buoyancy may take the form of air-bags or blocks of polystyrene foam.

When buying a new boat, with the expressed intention of using it in surf, it is always well advised to ask the manufacturer for the join or seam to be strengthened and reinforced. With large waves con-

stantly breaking over the deck it sustains, in general terms, more stresses than other parts of the craft.

Personal equipment again should be of the highest quality and its subsequent care and maintenance cannot be overstressed.

The spray deck needs to be tight-fitting and capable of withstanding the volume of water that is going to drop on it. A well-constructed neoprene deck is probably the best although sometimes they can be somewhat restricting. The recently introduced 'lifedecks', part plastic and part neoprene, with in-built buoyancy, would seem to be practical for surf canoeing.

The hoary argument of lifejacket versus buoyancy aid slots in naturally at this point but, for numerous and obvious reasons, has to be avoided. Suffice to say — one or the other must be worn and, whichever it might be, has to be respected and carefully maintained. Used as a cushion or pillow, throwing it scudding across a sandy beach or rocky shore, are all sure ways of shortening its life-saving capacity.

Wetsuits have an increasing number of loyal adherents but a paddler, at the novice stage, would be advised not to rush into purchasing one, but rather decide to what extent and where he will paddle and then seek expert advice on the best type and model for his own requirements. It is as well to remember that in cold weather they are a useful piece of protective clothing whilst in warm weather they can become uncomfortable and restricting.

During warmer weather a nylon canoeing jacket with neoprene cuffs and neck-band is probably the most suitable — yet there are even times when that might, in some countries, be wholly unnecessary.

Paddles are probably the most personalized piece of equipment the paddler will have. This is one area in which the novice is strongly urged to take advice. Much, obviously, will depend upon the degree of involvement in the sport but the by-word must be 'the best you can afford.'

Before moving on, mention must be made of the 'surf shoe' which is a very specialized surf canoe. It is distinguished by being flat-bottomed and having a small aft deck with the cockpit set well back. This type of construction allows it to be balanced more easily on a wave and, with the boat having a flat bottom, it is possible to spin it through 360° on the water's surface. This is definitely a boat for the advanced paddler and the connoisseur.

Canoe polo

There is a delightful old picture in a newspaper of the time showing men playing what is described as 'water polo' at Hunter's Quay in Scotland back in 1880. Men in striped bathing suits sit astride barrels that have toylike horses' heads and tails nailed on them and are playing polo by batting a ball about with their Rob Roy paddles. It cannot have been long before these gentlemen realized that it was easier to move around in a kayak rather than sit precariously on barrels that tended to roll over easily. However, the sharp prows of the kayaks of the day were too dangerous for the new sport to thrive. The canvas walls were easily torn or holed and the sport died out. It was only when fibreglass boats were developed, especially the smooth-nosed bath trainers, that canoe polo appeared again.

Once paddlers were in a swimming pool learning how to roll or to wiggle, they soon found that an amusing diversion was to scoop a water polo ball about. A target was devised and, hey presto!, rules were formulated and a team sport was born. Called BAT polo at first, because Bath Advanced Trainers were used, the first competition of note was as recent as 1979 when Oliver Cock set up an inter-city tournament in London. By staging this during the annual Canoe Exhibition, thousands of visiting

paddlers were exposed to the idea and embraced it enthusiastically.

The British Canoe Union set up a Rules Committee that both standardized the rules and injected some skill and safety to the game. The sport is still developing, so the rules are constantly being reviewed.

While the idea of playing indoors, or at least, in a swimming pool, has spread round the English-speaking world, a bigger version has developed in Germany. This is played on lakes and is a giant version of 'human' water polo. Water polo goals are used and the craft tend to be longer to suit the larger 'field' of play. Meanwhile in North America another version, based on the European concept, has sprung up. The game is played on open water rather than in a swimming pool, but differs from the game in Europe in that 'the ball must be passed, caught and shot with the hands; the paddles, taped to cover any sharp edges, are used only for stroking the water.'

The first national contest was held on 5 July 1980 at Nautahala Outdoor Centre.

Normally the game is played between two teams of five, though more or less can play for fun. The line-up is rather like a five-a-side soccer team with two defenders and three attackers. The defenders may well take it in turn to play in or near the goal, while the fastest paddler acts as the 'central striker', ready to sprint up the pool to collect the ball at the start of the match. Just as in soccer or basketball, there is a premium on accurate passing, and careful possession play, looking for openings in the defence. Both men and women play the game, where both paddles and the hands are used to propel both the ball and the boats about. The goal is a board, one metre square, two metres above the edge of the pool. By reading the rules, it becomes clear that the game has drawn on five-a-side soccer, water polo and handball, and can be more exciting than all three.

Whether played under Federation or local rules it is essential, with boats and paddles moving about rapidly, that smooth-tipped blades are used, and crash helmets and buoyancy aids should always be worn. The paddles are used for pushing or flicking the ball, never to hit it, and never when the ball is in an opponent's hands. As players must release the ball after five seconds (German rules) or three seconds (British rules) there is no need for violent tackles, though pushing an opponent's shoulder is allowed.

Ideally, a pass should go straight into a team mate's hands, or just in front of him so that he can swim to the ball and scoop it out of the water while

moving. As in so many team games, the hardest part of the rules to interpret is obstruction. It is obviously tactically sound to get between the paddler with the ball and his or her team mates in order to cut out a pass. However, it is forbidden to prevent an opponent from reaching the ball by deliberately blocking his or her way . . . so the play tends to flow and the action is thrilling for both spectators and participants.

Systems of play

Success at canoe polo depends very largely on the fitness and dedication of the competing teams and upon the organization and planning within the team.

a) Five players
   1. Goal keeper
   2. Defender
   3. Two 'midfield' players — one primarily defensive, one primarily attacking.
   4. Forward
b) Five players
   1. Goal keeper
   2. Two defenders
   3. Two attackers

The following are the rules of canoe polo:

1. Area of play Any shape and size of water, but goals will face each other and be between 20 and 30 metres apart. Goals will consist of a square with 1 metre sides supported vertically with the lower edge 2 metres above the water surface. 'Out of play' areas will be defined on each pitch.

2. Ball Size 5 plastic football, 27-28 inch circumference. Juniors — Size 4 plastic football.

3. Number of players Five each side. Players may be of either sex. Substitutes are allowed only for injury, and may not assist the players in any way. Substitutions may be made between games in a tournament providing that the substitute has not played for another team.

4. One referee, one umpire and a time keeper. The time keeper to keep the score and to blow for half-time and full-time. The time keeper shall be responsible for adding on time for injury, time wasting etc. on the instruction of the referee.

5. Boats Length — not less than 2 metres, and not more than 3 metres. Beam — not less than 50 cm and not more than 60 cm. Bow and stern plan — a curve at any point not less than 5 cm radius. Bow and stern profile — a curve at any point not less than 5 cm radius.

6. Propulsion By hand or paddle, single or double bladed.

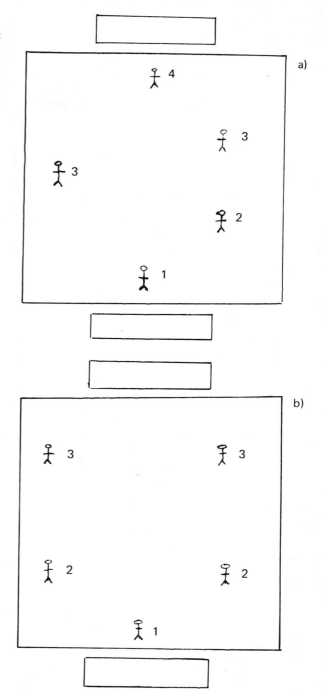

89 Systems of attack in canoe polo.

88 *(Left)* **Tackling an opponent in canoe polo** *(JAB Photos).*

7. Blades Must not be metal-tipped, and no part of the blade may have a radius of less than 3 cm in plan. Thin section GRP or ABS blades are not acceptable. Padding of metal tips is not allowed. Referees will disallow the use of blades which they consider to be dangerous.

8. Play Will not be more than seven and not less than four minutes each way. Injury time may be allowed.

9. Tie In this event, decision will be reached by taking the following steps in order.

 a) A one-minute interval and change of ends followed by play to the first goal. In the event of insufficient time to obtain a goal:

 b) Goal average.

 c) Goals conceded.

 d) Toss up. (It is hoped that this should never be necessary.)

10. Players Will wear team bibs or some easily identified team marking.

11. Players Will wear suitable helmets and buoyancy aids or belts which afford protection to the lower lumbar region.

12. All teams Must be ready to enter the water as the referee requests.

13. At the commencement of play, players will line up with their boats on their own goal line. The ball will be placed in the middle of the playing area. Play commences when the whistle is blown.

14. After half-time and after a goal is scored, the positions in Rule 13 will be taken.

15. a) When the ball is put out of play over the side line the non-offending team throws it in from the point of exit, but may not throw it in the direction of attack. Where there is a 'line' on the water the ball is out of play if it passes wholly over that line or where that line should be. If the poolside is used for 'out of bounds' then the ball is out of play if it touches the side of the pool.

 b) When the ball is put out of play over a goal line by an attacker the defending team has a goal throw from under the goal board. When the ball is put out of play over a goal line by a defender, the attacking team has a corner throw. The player taking the corner should be stationary in his canoe, parallel to the pool side.

 c) No goal can be scored from a penalty throw, goal throw or corner throw before the ball touches another player or his equipment.

 d) For any of the above throws there must be a space of at least 3 metres between the thrower and his nearest opponent. There should be 3 metres between the body of the thrower and the nearest

part of the opponent's body, paddle or canoe.

 e) The player taking a goal throw, corner throw or penalty throw may not play the ball a second time until it has touched another player or his equipment.

16. a) The paddle may be used for propulsion of the canoe, to stop or deflect the ball in the air or to draw the ball on the surface of the water. It may not be used to strike the ball either in the air or on the water. A strike takes place when a *positive* movement of the paddle causes the ball to change its direction by more than 90°. Special allowance may be made when a defender strikes the ball in defence of his goal.

 b) Deliberate or dangerous misuse of the paddle will be severely penalized. This includes making an attempt for the ball with the paddle while an opposition member is using his hand.

 c) If, in defence, a defending paddle is forced by the ball onto the goal, a goal is deemed to have been scored.

 d) An opposing player may not place his paddle within arm's length of a player who has the ball in his hand.

17. If a player leaves his canoe, he will be out of play until he is properly back in his canoe again.

18. If a player goes out of the playing area, he will be out of play until he returns to the area completely with no part of his craft over the boundary line.

19. A player may tackle only the man who is in possession of the ball. When the player has lost the ball the tackle must cease. A tackle can be made only by pushing the opponent's shoulder by the hand or arm. A player is in possession of the ball when he is in a position to play it with his hand, the ball being on the water and not in the air.

20. Obstructive play, removal of spray deck, attempts at sinking or holding under or any other form of play judged to be dangerous or unwanted will be penalized. If the bow or stern of a canoe makes contact with some force into the side of an opponent's canoe then the player shall be penalized for ramming. If a player wishing to move into a space is blocked by an opposing player then that player is obstructing. If one canoe passes onto another canoe then that canoe is obstructing. A player placing his paddle or arm over an opponent's canoe is obstructing.

21. A player must dispose of the ball within five seconds of handling it, whilst it is in play, either by passing the ball to another player or by throwing it at least one metre in any direction. If a player loses possession of the ball his five seconds shall begin again once he has regained clear possession. A player has not handled the ball until some part of his body or clothing has touched it.

22. Penalties will be at the discretion of the referee, these being as follows:

    a) Free throw to other side (see Rule 15c and d)

    b) Player sent off for two minutes or until the next goal.

    c) Player sent off for the rest of the match.

    d) Player referred to the Canoe Polo Executive for decision.

23. The referee may play 'advantage' if neither referee nor umpire blows his whistle and his decision is made clear.

24. Referee and umpire have authority.

Referee signals

Half-time	— Long blast on whistle.
Full-time	— Long blast on whistle.
Goal	— Whistle blast, both hands point to centre of pool.
Throw-in	— One hand points to where ball went out — second hand points in the direction the paddler taking the throw is attacking.
Goal throw	— One hand points to goal — second hand points in the direction the throw is to be taken.
Corner	— Both hands point to the corner.
Penalty throw	— One hand points in the direction in which the team taking the throw is attacking.

Hints If you intend to blow the whistle, blow it hard and make your decision clear. Blow the whistle before throwing in the ball at the start.

Signals for penalty throws

1. Foul tackle — Demonstrate foul (e.g. holding).
2. Obstruction — One arm raised high in the air.
3. Ramming — Push fist into open palm.
4. Five seconds — Raise five fingers.
5. Three metres — Raise three fingers.
6. Striking ball with paddle — Striking action with hands as if holding a paddle.
7. Dangerous use of a paddle — Chopping action of one hand on arm.
8. Advantage — Wave 'play on' with both hands.

After 1-7 above, the appropriate signal to clarify where the infringement occured and the direction of the throw should be given.

Canoe sailing

The idea of sailing a canoe is as old as organized canoeing itself. When John MacGregor was touring, he often set a lugsail, so that he could make full use of any wind. Friends of his, including Warrington Baden-Powell (brother of the founder of the Boy Scout movement), developed the sailing side of canoeing to such an extent that there was a section of the Canoe Club devoted to 'sail racing'. At first, the canoe sailing boat was merely a canoe with a mast set in the foredeck. Sometimes another small sail was added in the aftdeck. The idea of a centre-board was introduced by the Americans and the sailor was able to keep warm and dry inside his kayak as he trimmed his sails enjoying an ingeniously designed set of ropes. The sport was so popular that a challenge trophy was put up by the Royal Canoe Club in 1874, and twelve years later the New York Canoe Club's International Challenge Cup attracted entries from Britain.

From then on, canoe sailing found itself in a quandary as many innovations made the craft involved more like a fast, narrow two-man dinghy than a canoe. For one thing, the Americans found that they could go faster by sitting *on* the deck rather than under it. In this way, the body could be better used as a counterbalance when a strong wind heeled the boat over. Next came sliding seats, so that the sailor could lean out even further as a counterbalance. Clearly, canoe sailing was already just another form of sailing, yet the sport has remained under the wing of the International Canoe Federation, rather than the International Yacht Union, to which many think it should now be transferred.

The course An equilateral triangle marked by three buoys. Sailed in order: start, 1, 2, 3, 1, 3, 1, 2, 3, finish. The number 1 buoy is always set to windward of the start. Each leg of the course is about $1\frac{1}{8}$ nautical miles, giving a total distance of about 10 nautical miles.

Start and finish lines are between the buoys and the foremast of the race committee boat (which flies a blue flag when it is on station).

If the course is shortened, the race usually finishes at the number 1 buoy, giving a total distance of about 6½ nautical miles.

Officials Race committee, protest committee, measurement committee.

Protests and appeals Protests are made as in the IYRU rules. Appeals against decisions by protest or measurement committees are decided by the ICF Sailing Committee.

Wind speed Normally races are not started in winds faster than 10 metres per second.

Time limits Races are void if the first canoe fails to complete: the first round within 1 hour 20 minutes;

90 Canoe sailing during the world championships, Hayling Island (*G. Mackereth*).

the whole course within 4 hours; the shortened course at an average speed of 2½ knots.

Scoring system First place, ¾ point; second place, 2 points; third place, 3 points; and so on. Retirement, maximum plus 1 point. Non-starter, maximum plus 2. Disqualification, maximum plus 3. (Maximum is the number of competitors attending the championships, after withdrawals.)

The lowest scorer wins.

If six or seven races are held, each competitor may discard his score for one race.

If less than five races are held, the championship is annulled.

Class rules All boats must be officially measured and receive certificates of conformity to class rules. These aim to make hull shapes and sail areas as uniform as possible. There are no restrictions on deck layout or sail plan.

Remeasurement is required after extensive modifications or repairs. Canoes first measured before 1 January 1971 must conform to rules in force at

that time; repairs must conform to the same rules, and major reconstruction to present rules.

10sq m canoe Length: 5.180 m (17 ft); Beam: 1.018 m (3 ft 4 in); Minimum weight: 63 kg (139 lb)
Centreboard must not project more than 1 m from the underside of the hull. It must be fixed in case of capsize and be capable of being fully raised so as not to project beyond the keel.

Sliding seat Maximum extension: 1.525 m either side of the canoe. Weight: 9-12 kg, including moving parts.

Carriage must not extend beyond the sheerline.
Hull Any material or method of construction may be used. Must be to drawn design, within tolerances allowed for minor errors and ageing.

Mast, boom, rigging Rotating masts: maximum thickness at least $\frac{2}{3}$ of the depths at the same position. Gaffs and permanently curved masts and spars are forbidden. No sail may be set more than 6.36 m above the underside of the hull. (Maximum height of the foretriangle: 4.73 m above the underside of the hull, where the line of the forestay meets the foward surface of the mast.)

Sails Total area: maximum of 10 sq m. Mainsail

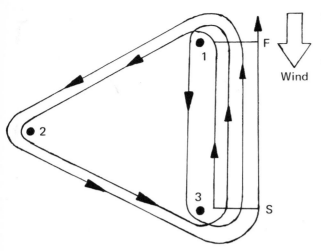

91 Sailing course.

area: maximum of 8.5 sq m.

Sails must be of woven material and be able to be stored in sail bags of a prescribed size.

A sail window of non-woven material must not exceed 60 cm in any dimension. Letters IC in red, national letter, and registered number must be carried on the mainsail.

Crew One person.

Dress Personal buoyancy aid must be worn or carried ready for use.

Hull buoyancy 75 kg mimimum with hull flooded. Must be at least two tanks or flexible bags.

Measurements are checked with templates. The hull is completely decked and unswampable. Protective strips on the keel and centreboard are not included in measurements. Rubbing bands at the gunwales must be of certain dimensions. Stripped weight to be at least 63 kg (maximum of 5 kg correcting weights).

The first world championship was held in Stockholm in 1938, based on the popular European style craft that carried 7½ square metres of sail. When the Swedes won this, they were challenged to try their luck against the Anglo-American 10-square-metre boats. Racing at Hayling Island in 1939, the Swedes were trounced by the Royal Canoe Club's experts and after the Second World War, when the ICF was founded, it adopted the sailing canoe with the 10-square-metre sail known as the IC (International Canoe) class.

Further designs in both the United States and Britain made the IC faster and faster, helped by the introduction of new materials such as GRP hulls, aluminium masts and nylon sheets and sails. Now-

adays sailing canoes are the fastest single-hull dinghies afloat.

Rules

The course sailed in international competitions is based on the Olympic triangular course. Points are calculated on the basis of seven races. Competitors can discard their worst result and the lower scorer wins. A first place scores ¾ point; second, 2; third, 3 and so on. There is no paddling involved, and all the techniques and tactics involved relate directly to dinghy sailing.

92 10 sq metre canoe.

North American canoeing

The Canadian canoe is a unique boat. Its design evolved on a continent with numerous lakes and rivers. The boat had to be big enough to transport people and goods, yet small enough to carry over portage trails between lakes and around rapids. Early canoes were dug or burned out of logs. Other designs included spreading skins on a wood frame, and using birch-bark. Bark canoes were light, durable, and were used by many of the Indian tribes and early explorers of the North American continent. In fact most of the early exploration and commercial development of North America would not have been possible without the canoe. The French missionary, Jacques Marquette, used canoes during the mid-seventeenth century to explore and discover a waterway from the St Lawrence River in Ontario to the Gulf of Mexico. In the eighteenth century, Sir Alexander MacKenzie used canoes for his epic exploration trips. MacKenzie, born in Scotland, emigrated to the United States in the mid-1700s and worked for the Hudson Bay Company in Canada. His longest trip was from Lake Athabaska down the Slave River to the Great Slave Lake, and then down the MacKenzie River (named after Sir Alexander) to the Arctic Ocean. Over 1300 miles long, this trip down uncharted and unexplored waters would be the equivalent of a trip down a wild, unknown river from Amsterdam to Gibraltar.

Canoes were essential to the development of the fur trade in North America, and early commercial development was controlled by the French. However, after 1760 the English controlled Canada where the Hudson Bay Company was the major trading company on the continent. After the break-up of the ice each spring Canadian voyageurs would leave Montreal and paddle up the Great Lakes to Grand Portage on the western end of Lake Superior. There they would meet the voyageurs who came from Lake Athabaska and the other lakes of the Canadian north-west bringing beaver skins and other furs for the European fur market. The voyageurs were tough, wiry men with a legendary *joie de vivre*. One voyageur well past 70 years of age was quoted as saying:

I could carry, paddle, walk and sing with any man I ever saw. I have been twenty-four years a canoe man, and forty-one years in the service; no portage was ever too long for me. Fifty songs could I sing. I have saved the lives of ten voyageurs. Have had twelve wives and six running dogs. I spent all my money in pleasure. Were I young again, I should spend my life the same way over. There is no life so happy as a voyageur's life.

Until the development of the large river boats and railroads, the canoe played a dominant role in the exploration and commercial development of the North American continent.

In the twentieth century the canoe has fulfilled many of the recreational needs of Canadians and Americans. Prior to the Second World War most canoes were made of canvas stretched on a wood frame, a technique which would have been understandable to Indian canoe builders. Since the Second World War, however, new materials and designs have been developed. High aluminium alloy was used extensively in the 1950s to create a boat of medium weight (85 pounds), high durability, and no maintenance. In the 1960s fibreglass materials came into use, resulting in lighter weight but less durable boats. In the 1970s synthetic materials have been bonded together to produce a material known as ABS, marketed under the trade name Royalex. This material, which is vinyl on the outside, slides easily over rocks and other obstacles in rivers, but is reasonably light in weight (approximately 70 pounds). Its most novel feature is its 'memory'.

ABS canoes have been seen completely wrapped around rocks under water in a river, with the bow and stern touching each other on the downstream side of the rock. When the canoe has been pulled out of the river, it pops back into its original shape, leaving only a few wrinkles in the skin of the canoe. The cost of canoes vary widely from 400 dollars for an aluminium canoe to 600 dollars for ABS, and as much as 800 dollars for a wood-and-canvas boat.

With the development of tougher, more durable materials, white water canoeing has increased in popularity. White water enthusiasts can be found in the north-eastern United States where rivers and streams drop precipitously out of the mountains on their way to the ocean. White water rivers are graded according to an international river classification system:

Class I Easy. Waves small, and regular. Passages clear.

Class II Medium. Rapids of medium difficulty, with passages clear and wide; waves up to 2 feet high.

Class III Moderately difficult. Waves numerous, irregular and up to 3 feet high; numerous rocks and eddies. Rapids with passages that are narrow, requiring expertise in manoeuvre; inspection usually needed.

Class IV Difficult. Long rapids with powerful, irregular waves up to 4½ feet high; dangerous rocks and boiling eddies; channels very narrow and twisted; inspection mandatory for the first time; powerful and precise manoeuvring required.

Class V Very difficult. Extremely difficult, long and very violent rapids following each other almost without interruption; river bed extremely obstructed;

large drops of 4½ feet and irregular 5-foot waves.

Canoeists in New England in the 1950s and 60s generally contented themselves with Class II or Class III rapids. Class IV and Class V were reserved for kayakers and covered canoes. However, improvements in canoe design and technique in the 1970s has developed a new class of open boat canoeists, willing to tackle any white water river. Class IV rapids, which were listed in guidebooks as 'unrunnable gorges' in 1968, and were attempted only by kayakers, are now run on a regular basis by canoeists. Canoeists have even successfully negotiated 10-foot waterfalls on some New England rivers.

For the white water enthusiast in New England, the spring provides the greatest opportunity. Warm April breezes melt the ice and snow on the mountains and swell the flow of rivers and streams. Canoeing begins with snow on the banks, and often ice flows along the banks of the rivers. Canoeists wear wetsuits when doing spring boating. These rubber suits are made of ¼ inch rubber and cover the entire body

93 An open Canadian canoe, as used in North America, shooting a rapid (*Wade*).

except for the hands, neck and head. Add a helmet and lifejacket to the boater, mix in air temperatures of 40° F and a light snow, and you will have an accurate picture of a typical New England white water run in late March or early April.

After the spring run-off, white water paddlers find little amusement except for releases from some of the dams on New England rivers. Over 10,000 dams have been built on New England rivers, and many of them are managed by the US Army Corps of Engineers for flood control purposes. In the summer and fall, the Corps releases water from these dams, often providing white water canoeing in a more pleasurable climate.

In white water canoeing, the bowman reigns supreme. Being 15 feet ahead of the sternman and able to quickly effect the course of the canoe, the bowman must have good judgement and reflexes and must be able to 'read the water' by seeing a course through the rocks which will avoid the canoe hitting a rock or going into a hole so big that the water comes over the side and sinks the boat. The sternman's job is to anticipate and complement the actions of the bowman. Is is more important to think alike than to be good paddlers when paddling double through open waters. A poorly matched team will have different instincts in a given situation, resulting in the bowman and sternman pulling in opposite directions, and the canoe going through the rapids broadside, ending up on a rock or underwater.

Of course, not all American paddlers prefer the thrills and chills of white water canoeing. Many still enjoy the adventure of an expedition trip, carrying the tent, sleeping bag, and food in the canoe. In the early 1930s a young man from Minnesota made a 2200-mile trip in an 18-foot canoe from Minneapolis, Minnesota, to Hudson Bay. The trip took over four months and resulted in a book being published describing the trip. The young man later became a well known American reporter and television commentator — Eric Sevareid. For those who cannot afford a four-month vacation, a weekend or week-long expedition trip provides an unusual opportunity to get away from the hectic pace of day-to-day life, and renew one's relationship with the natural world. On each expedition trip there is a special moment when the canoeist pushes away from the beach or dock, takes the paddle in his hand, and looks out across the lake or river. At that moment, carrying with him whatever he will need, the canoeist comes as close to a feeling of self-sufficiency from modern society as is possible to get. It is a feeling also experienced by backpackers and sailors, but rarely in a boat so small and fragile as a canoe.

On a flat water trip, the roles of bowman and sternman are reversed. The bowman provides the power stroke, and the sternman sets the course. The sternman must make small corrections to the course on each stroke, using a pry or a draw stroke to gently keep the boat on course. Canoeists develop a rhythm for paddling which can be maintained for hours at a time. Going down lakes or broad rivers, a headwind is often encountered, making progress much slower. However, on the rare occasions when a tailwind

blows, canoes often raft together and sail, using the fly from a tent, a canvas tarp, or other suitable sail cloth. Canoeists can often make 20 to 25 miles in a good day down lakes and rivers, provided that there are no portages.

Portages! The bane of a canoeist's existence. Most portages are measured in yards. The memorable ones are measured in miles. Grand Portage, used by the Canadian voyageurs to go from Lake Superior around the rapids of the Pigeon river, was 9 miles long. In order to carry the canoe and other gear across portages, several methods are used. The canoe is often carried by tying the paddles on to the middle thwart and bow seat. The canoeist then flips the canoe upside down and holds it on his shoulders with the broad part of the paddle spreading the weight over each shoulder evenly. An 80-pound canoe can be carried for several miles this way. Dried food and other supplies are carried in either soft canvas packs called 'Duluth' packs, named after the section of Michigan and Minnesota which developed them, or in wooden boxes called 'wannigans' (an Indian term for 'wooden box'). A leather strap called a 'tumpline' is wrapped around the wannigan which is then carried on the back of the canoeist with the tumpline going over the middle of the head. Seventy or 80 pounds of supplies can be carried in this way over a portage trail. With the development of freeze-dried foods and other weight-saving devices, the weight required for a 3 to 7 day trip has been substantially reduced. However, portages still are just plain hard work and have few redeeming features. It is always a happy moment in a canoeist's day when the first glimmer of blue water shows through the trees at the end of a portage trail.

Of course, canoes are used for many activities other than family picnic outings, sailing and fishing. Water-skiing has even been attempted, without notable success! Because the canoe's design combines stability with shallow draft (2-3 inches), it is an excellent fishing boat on waters as diverse as deep lakes and shallow streams. In fact, its wide popularity can be attributed in large part to its versatility. For many people and particularly families who are buying their first boat, the Canadian canoe is the logical answer.

CHAPTER 10

The International Scene and Interviews with Two Champions

Racing round the world

Throughout the international calendar there are a number of events which are 'classics' or are on the way to being so — classic because they have something more in their make-up other than being straight forwardly competitive.

Many of them are over long distances and attract a great deal of interest because of the wide spectrum of paddler who takes part — the Devizes-Westminster attracts many tourists who do the race just to say they have completed it, whilst others are all out to win.

The Gudena Marathon is characterized by the number of classes which cater for every category of paddler, in Kayaks 1, 2 and Canadian canoes, from international class down to the most humble of club paddlers and veterans.

So, throughout the world, from Gudena in Denmark, via the St Lawrence River in Canada, to the River Sella in Spain, back to The Liffey in Ireland and then on to the Blue Water Classic, in Australia, there are events which stimulate interest in this ever-growing and expanding sport.

Devizes to Westminster (England)

Many marathon races claim to be the toughest in the world, but one of the strongest contenders must be the Devizes to Westminster Race, which is mainly down the River Thames in England. Each year some 300 paddlers spend the Easter weekend racing over 125 miles. The Seniors do the race non-stop, right through the night, which makes it even more gruelling than most marathons. Juniors stop overnight.

What makes this race different is that there is no mass start, competitors can start where they choose in order to take advantage of the tidal part of the Thames below Teddington Lock. Proposed start times are revealed only to officials, so the favourites try to look unconcerned as they come up to the start time that they think will bring them most benefit further down the river. A team that starts too late could leave itself too much to do; a team that reaches the tideway before the tide has changed will have to work harder than expected. There are no fewer than 76 locks to be negotiated by the K2s with short portages at each, so training to run with the canoe is an important factor.

Devizes is a quiet little town in Wiltshire that finds itself invaded by paddlers, but everyone co-operates to send the competitors safely on their way. Support teams race ahead ready to thrust hot or cold drinks, candy bars or even hot cooked food into their team's hands. After 15 miles, the paddlers have to leave the canal to portage across a busy road bridge, remembering to shout out the number of their canoe to the officials. A local police-man devotes 56 hours of his own time to stopping traffic at Wootton Rivers to allow the paddlers to hog the road.

Only 4 miles further on at Crofton Locks a mile-long portage tests inexperienced paddlers severely, coming so soon after the start. Crews who paddle as far as Reading have already notched up 52 miles. They leave the Kennet and Avon Canal and are then on the Thames itself.

The race has to take place early in the year, before the thick weeds clog up the canal. However, Easter in England is notorious for its bad weather and first aid experts have treated paddlers for both frostbite and heatstroke in the 30 odd years since the event began in 1949.

Marlow is a picturesque riverside village in the Thames Valley about 70 miles from Devizes, but the top paddlers see none of the beauty and feel only the pain as they struggle on, desperate to catch the tide at Teddington. Any delay could leave them the impossible task of paddling against the tide . . . and they could be held up for six hours.

The winners rarely stop for sustenance, relying on their own food and drink in the canoe, thereby

94 The Sella Race, Spain (*Juan Feliz*).

saving precious seconds. Amazingly, they average about 8 miles per hour, covering the 124.31 miles in an exhausting 16 hours.

Since they set off at different times, competitors reach the finishing line of Westminster Bridge, near Big Ben, at all times of the day and night. There is no huge crowd awaiting them, no cheer goes up as the line is crossed. Canoeing is a sport for loners and the Devizes to Westminster is the ultimate test for this rare breed.

The Sella (Spain)

Another famous competition that attracts paddlers from all over the world is the Sella Descent. On the first Saturday in August each year hundreds of canoeists flock to the province of Asturias in north-west Spain for one of the oldest and most famous down river races — the Sella. Starting in Arriondas, famous for its slalom, the idea is to follow the twisting River Sella with its shallow but rapid water. Seniors, Juniors and Veterans cover 19 kilometres while Cadets and Ladies race only 10 kilometres.

The race, like so many long distance races, was the development of a friendly outing. Dionisio de la Huerta's idea in 1930 now attracts over 300,000 spectators and representatives of about 20 nations to the rugged but beautiful countryside where many camp on the river bank. The event takes place in a carnival atmosphere with locals in fancy dress, wearing masks. At about 10 in the morning, everyone flocks through the town to the sound of bagpipes which are native to the region. Garlands of flowers, funny hats, music and laughter — all ensure that this is a unique occasion.

Competitors are part of this parade, carrying their paddles as they make their way to the bridge at Arriondas. Already their boats — K1, K2, C1, C2 and RR — are drawn up on the shore, their places decided by lot. The tension mounts as the national anthems of each country are played. Finally, 'Asturias patria querida' (Asturias, beloved father-land) is played and the crowd joins in the singing that signals the approaching start. A loud shot rings out and the race is on.

On the face of it, the course is not difficult or dangerous as its rapids are rated only Class I and Class II. It is the sheer numbers battling it out that make it such an intriguing contest. As crews try to get ahead of the pack there are collisions; some boats face the wrong way; some capsize. Unpleasant as that may be for the participants, it is hugely amusing for the crowds on the bank, who have been tuning their voices with a pitcher or two of sangria or the local cider.

As if the scene were not unusual enough, there is a special train that chugs slowly down the left-hand side of the course affording a spendid view of the action and stopping from time to time to let passengers off. They dash down to the river's edge to watch the leaders pass before scrambling back on board at the impatient sound of the train's whistle.

The main road along the right-hand bank is closed off for most of the day to accommodate the cavalcade of buses that also follows the race. There is almost as much drama on the road as there is in the Sella.

For the competitors, the river is fairly flat with broad, pebbled strand and deep green pools favoured by the salmon on either side. The valley itself is farming country with orchards, corn fields and meadows that are dotted with horreos, granaries that stand on stone legs above the ground.

Although the riverbed is strewn with boulders, the mainstream is fast and deep, but narrow. The struggle, therefore, is not only to stay in front but also in the best water.

Spectators are already thronging the town of Ribadesella at the end of the course, making it impossible to park. They are thickest on the bridge over the river as this marks the finish. One of the stone plinths has previous winners carved on it and flies the flag of the previous year's winner. The winning time is usually about 1 hour 20 minutes and the winner is feted in a specially decorated canoe, with all the contestants taking to the water again, heading for the meadows of Ova, near the village of Llovio. There, 3 kilometres below Ribadesella, there is a huge picnic and prizegiving . . . but that's not the end of the festivities. Back in Ribadesella the party goes on in Spanish-style late into the night.

The Pontevedra (Spain)

Another Spanish race that is growing in status is the Pontevedra Race which actually starts at the village of Portonovo on the rocky northern shore of the Pontevedra estuary. Starting at 6 p.m., about 300 paddlers, all in K4s, leave in a mass start from a half-moon beach. A hooter goes off, accompanied by a crackle of fireworks. Then the difficulties begin because a sprint K4 is not designed for sea water. The swell picks up the long boats and can throw them against each other. In the waves, the bow often plunges 6 feet underwater, and the stroke paddler can find himself chest-deep in the water which inevitably seeps in under his spray covers. Foot pumps are needed and it is not unusual to see boats sinking or even snapping in half!

As the kayaks hug the shore, this is all enter-tainment for the big crowds that line the rocky cliff edge. Eventually the paddlers reach the calmer waters of the Lerez River and follow the motor boat that leads the way, up to the bridge which is the finishing line in Pontevedra. It takes about an hour and a half.

The Gudena (Denmark)

Although the Devizes to Westminster Race is a severe test of stamina involving innumerable portages, the Gudena Race in Denmark always attracts the

95 Alan 'Willy' Williams and John Fowler during the Gudena Race, Denmark (*Graham Ingram-Monk*).

best marathon paddlers in the world. A combination of the best of the Sella and the Devizes to Westminster, the Gudena starts in Skanderborg south of Arhus and arcs round to Randers, with an overnight stop at Silkeborg. The course crosses lakes and follows the Gudena River before finishing in the estuary.

Spread over two days, the first day covers about 35 miles in two stages split by a mandatory 40-minute break and includes crossing Lake Mossa which can be very rough when there is a headwind. The second day has three sectors consisting of a 21-mile leg, followed by a 40-minute break, then 18 miles (20-minute break) and the final 10 miles into Randers.

The river is quite twisty, providing a deepwater race with little or no white water and apart from the lakes it can often be quite narrow, only 50 to 60 feet across. The prestige event is the K1, featuring about 250 entries, but there are also K2 and touring classes.

Including entrants for a short course race for C1, well over 1000 competitors take part. Support crews can get to the paddlers only at the stop-overs which are sometimes thought to be more trouble than they are worth, as paddlers tend to stiffen physically and over relax psychologically. In 40 minutes, however, there is scarcely time to lift the boat out, get the wet gear off, put dry clothes on, and grab something to eat before setting off again.

The International Canoe Classic (Canada)

In North America, marathon racing is attracting more and more spectators as well as competitors. Not surprisingly, this has attracted sponsorship and prize money. One popular race is the International Canoe Classic worth 1600 dollars to the winner which take splace on Labor Day weekend, at the end of the summer. Covering 100 miles from La Tuque to Trois Rivieres on the St Lawrence River, the canoes follow the St Maurice River. Well over 100 canoes, known as 3 x 27s because they are 27 inches wide at the 3-inch waterline, take part and some 500,000 spectators not only watch but dance and enjoy the festivals that go on along the river bank. On the first day the going is quite easy, though the paddlers are in action for 7 hours on the water, but the second day there are three tough portages, one of over a mile, and two of half a mile. This day lasts 4½ hours and includes two special sections in the middle and at the end which are sprints. These are races within the race, with special prizes for the winners. The third day is about 3½ hours long with two half-mile portages and another spectacular sprint up to the finish.

The course passes the wild yet beautiful country of the Reserve du St Maurice and the Parc National de la Maurice before going through the quaintly named towns of Grand-Mere and Shawinigan. It is doubtful whether the paddlers have a chance to enjoy the view!

But not all races take place in the summer.

The Ice-Breaker Race (USA)

Imagine a cold, sunny November day with the temperature hovering at 40° F and a brisk wind blowing up a river outside Boston, Massachusetts. About 200 canoes, kayaks, and other assorted craft are lined up across the 30-yard river awaiting the starter's signal. At the sound of the gun, each boat springs forward, creating mass confusion and mayhem. War canoes with ten men paddling crack over slalom kayaks, family canoes collide, babies cry. Five miles downriver the boats have sorted themselves out and come across the finish line to the cheers of the crowd. Hot coffee, tea and doughnuts are passed around and many paddlers end up with a ribbon in their class. This is the Ice-Breaker Race on the Concord River, traditionally run on the first Sunday in November, and the last time that most paddlers put a paddle into water until the next spring run-off begins.

The Liffey (Ireland)

There are other classic marathon races such as the 28-kilometre Liffey Descent which finishes near Dublin in Ireland. With its nine huge weirs, its rapids and one particularly long portage, it presents a real challenge.

The Berg (South Africa)

In the second week of July each year, some 250 K1 competitors line up on the banks of the Berg River in Paarl to race 256 kilometres to Velddrif in South Africa's Western Province. Known as the Winelands Race because the river runs through the vineyards north of Cape Town, the race lasts four days with three overnight stops, and features Seniors, Juniors, Schoolboys and Ladies. Racing in South African winter, the river can present different conditions every year. In 1977 there was so much rain that the meanders disappeared completely at the lower end of the river and paddlers were able to cut straight across the loops. Even with a medium-height river there is only one portage and so the race suits the ultra-long-distance paddler, who can handle the sharp turns and bramble bushes on the Berg. There is a mass start each morning, though seeding puts the leaders in the front row on the bank. South Africa's other long distance race is the Pietermaritzberg to Durban Race which has been compared with the Devizes to Westminster as it has so many portages.

Australia

In Australia, there is the unusual Blue Water Classic. Only 1-mile long, it is an ocean race from Wollongong Harbour round to Wollongong Beach through strong swell and big waves. More traditional is the 100 miler on the Nepean River in New South Wales which is described as a 'paddle-a-thon' as it raises money for a local hospital. Held in late November or early December (summer in the Southern Hemisphere) on a weekend that coincides with the full moon, it is a non-stop event, on a circular course between Penrith and the Warragamba River Junction. Clergymen from three denominations bless the paddlers before the races start at 10.00 a.m. on Saturday morning.

Other events are the Port Hacking Classic near Sydney, which covers 7 miles and the Williams River Classic from Dungog to Clarencetown which has an overnight stop.

Interviews with two champions

Einar Rasmussen

Einar Rasmussen is one of the world's top paddlers. Twenty-two years of age, born in southern Norway, he now lives in Oslo. He first came to prominence internationally in 1975 when he won a gold medal at the World Championships in K4 10,000 metres. He represents all that is good about the modern canoeist, because he not only relishes competition but enjoys the relaxation of canoeing for recreation. At an international regatta held at Britain's National Water Sports Centre at Holme Pierrepont outside Nottingham he talked about his preparation and his attitude to competition.

Q: When you are racing on a special flat water course, what disturbs you more — wind or waves?

96 Norwegian silver medalist, Einar Rasmussen, in action (*Tore Kristiansen*).

A: Waves are the worst thing to deal with, because the kayak dips into them and you get a lot of water coming in. And when the nose dips it destroys the rhythm and the kayak slows dramatically. You can deal with the wind more easily. When it is head on, you shorten your stroke but maintain the same rhythm because you are travelling more slowly. It's harder for the muscles and your arms get stiff faster. When the wind is behind you, the kayak goes faster and its harder for your lungs and your heart. Then it's your body that gets tired, rather than your arms.

Q: Is it just the top part of your body that feels this?

A: No. You use the whole of your body, especially the stomach muscles and you try to rotate rather than use the arms too much. The Russians have fantastic technique; they keep their arms in the same position without bending them and use their rotational movement to propel the kayak forward.

Q: Does everyone imitate them?

A: No. The East Germans, for instance, are stronger and they *do* use their arms. These are the two approaches to paddling. I prefer the Russian technique but I think I end up somewhere in between. You could call it the Scandinavian way!

Q: If the East Germans use only their arms presumably they have to do a lot of training to strengthen the arm muscles.

A: Yes, they do a lot of weight training which makes them much stronger. Most of them are good sprinters though Rudiger Helm can paddle anything, including the 10,000 metres.

Q: What is the most obvious difference in the two styles?

A: As the East Germans use their arms they have a short and very strong pull. The Russians use their bodies and they turn a lot. Their strokes are very long and not so jerky.

Q: What other styles are there?

A: Well the Norwegians use a bit of both but we're looking mostly at the Russians because their style is both strong and smooth.

Q: What about the Hungarians? They had a great tradition of paddling. Have they got an old-fashioned style? Have people given that up now?

A: Yes, I think some Hungarians are a little bit old-fashioned but they have a new generation coming up.

Q: What about your own training? What sort of weight lifting training do you do off the water?

A: I don't normally train with weights. My weight training follows a paddling action. I work out for two hours every day, so even in winter I am 'paddling' for at least two hours every day.

Q: What sort of gadgetry do you use for that?

A: I have made my own machine in the cellar. It's a bar with weights attached to the end of a rope which I pull. It reproduces the same movement as being in a kayak; I have a paddle and I use an isotonic system, like the swimmers.

Q: But everyone agrees that it is vital to get out on the water as often as possible. You exercise in the cellar because there's snow outside, but would you rather be on the water?

A: Of course. I also do some weight training because you don't get strong enough just paddling. I will continue the weight training in summer, too. So I will be paddling, weight training and doing some running throughout the year. We used to do just one type of training in winter and another in spring but now it is more or less the same all the year round. The old method of getting in form no longer applies. I am always ready to race.

Q: You are a sprint kayak specialist, yet you also seem to enjoy marathon racing.

A: Yes, I think it is fun. So I've done the Gudena in Denmark twice as well as some long distance races in Norway like the Nøtterrund, the biggest touring race in Norway that goes round the islands in Tønsberg. I don't train for it, I just do them for fun. My real training is for 500 and 1000 metres.

Q: Apart from training, there are tactics in every race. What sort of plan do you follow when you go out?

A: We train so that we can do the maximum in a race so in training we find our correct speeds. For a 1000 metres we take the time every 250 metres, then we find out how fast we can paddle the whole distance. We aim to race at the same speed throughout except that the first 250 metres should be two seconds faster than the last three sections which should be in the same times, so that an even pace and rhythm are maintained. When we raced in the World Championships final we kept at the right pace and we won. If you can think that way, then you're more relaxed and you don't worry about the Russians and East Germans. You do your own thing!

Q: So this is contrary to the traditional tactic of starting fast then coasting before putting in a final sprint?

A: Yes. Everybody starts with a bang so we were sixth at the first 250 metres, then third at the 500 and 750 metres mark. But we were first at the finish! We just found our correct speed and rhythm and ignored the other competitors.

Q: By keeping just to one rhythm are you saving energy?

A: Yes. The theory is that you can't do better than your maximum so that's what you find. I have been talking about K2. Now I can apply that to K1. If there is a strong wind I have to allow for it. For example, I will think of opening with a 1 minute 50 second on the first 500 metres and a 3 minute 44 second for the 1000. That will give me my maximum. The Russian and the East

German paddlers will be there and all the other good paddlers. They do their best and I do my best. At the end I'll look across to see if I am Number 1 — or Number 9, but I'll know I have done my best.

Q: When do you look at your watch?

A: Never in a race, but when I'm training I use my watch all the time to try to find the correct speed.

Q: So you're training yourself to have a little clock inside your head?

A: Yes. I follow that and it helps calm the nerves. I relax because I know just what I have to do.

Q: Now you also race in a K2 and K4. Presumably everyone has to have the same paddling technique?

A: Yes, and that's one reason why the Russians have such a good K4 in the 1000 metres. They have the same technique so they can achieve a very good rhythm.

Q: There must be some teams where you can tell just by watching that they have learnt in different ways and therefore they won't be as quick.

A: Well, the English have problems there. They have many paddlers who are good individually but they have trouble combining to make a good K2 and especially K4 because some use the Russian method of paddling and others use the East German way. So the rhythm is wrong.

Q: Let's talk about the race itself. On the day, what time do you get up?

A: I have to get up 2½ hours before I race and I eat at once so that I have at keast two hours to digest afterwards.

Q: What sort of food do you eat?

A: Bread and cornflakes, carbohydrates really, then I relax after eating, to get my food digested. When you eat, all the blood goes to the stomach to help the digestion so you should let nature take its course. Then I try and concentrate for one hour before a race. I walk or jog and then 30 minutes before the start I get into the canoe and paddle slowly for five or six minutes. Then I do some sprints, not too hard. I'd do three one-minute bursts, resting for two minutes in between. Then I do a couple of 20 or 30 second sprints quite fast. The last 6 or 7 minutes before the start I just paddle and relax, trying not to think about the race, just relax. Sometimes I feel I am not nervous enough, perhaps when I am racing in Norway, so I try to concentrate to make myself nervous. I try to find the right feeling, I don't want to be too afraid but I do have to have butterflies in my stomach.

After a race if I get through to the final in the afternoon, I will paddle about 10 minutes to get rid of the lactic acid in my muscles and to relax. Then in the afternoon I use the same warm-up. It's very important to warm-up properly. It's good for concentration and you have a set programme for the last half hour before the race. Psychologically you have something to do and it steadies you.

Q: Is this a plan you worked out, or was it your coach? Or is it just experience?

A: It's everything. I change the programme a little every year. When I do well in a race I try to think what I did before that race so I can do it again next time.

Q: Once you're ready to race there must be various tricks of the trade, particularly at international level.

A: In the kayak we have an unusual start because when you hear 'ready', you start. We never hear 'go'. The preparatory signal is 'one minute left to the start' and then we all paddle up to the start. In the world championships someone holds the boats and they have headphones. But we don't hear 'go' because we have gone. If you do hear 'go' then you've had a bad start. It's a good system. You start on the first thing you hear from the starter. That's fair enough.

Q: What do the people with headphones do?

A: They are saying 'forward' or 'backward' to be exactly on the same line at the start. Then they just let go. Sometimes you say 'give us a push' — and we can feel it!

Q: Once you start you give big digs with the paddle.

A: Yes, for the first 10 or 15 metres you want to get the boat up to speed as fast as you can. Many paddlers go at full speed to keep in touch with the leader but, as I've explained, I try to find my correct speed and try to relax. The first 500, the first half of the distance, I try to go fast enough with the maximum relaxation. After half way if I've got a problem with my speed, I go harder and harder to keep it steady but the last 150 to 200 metres I forget everything about technique. Then it's pure fighting. You're stiff in the arms but you just go, go, go. There's no technique.

Q: Is it the arms that feel it most?

A: Yes.

Q: Do you find, like a runner, that the colour goes out of things, that you're so tired that you see just one little tunnel?

A: Sometimes, in some races. But sometimes you don't get tired at all, just stiff. Sometimes you don't know what's happened. You paddle and you don't know how you've done. Number 1 or Number 9, you just don't know.

Q: What do you think about at the start — the timing you want to achieve or the hard paddling at the beginning?

A: I think a lot about the technique. Sometimes I get a feeling that this will be a good race but sometimes after 100 metres I think it's going to be a terrible race.

Q: Once you start, if you are going badly, is it too late to correct it?

A: Yes, if it isn't your day and your body isn't ready for a good race, then that's it.

Q: Wouldn't you already realize that during your warm-up?

A: No, no. Sometimes I feel terrible during the warm-up. I feel sick. I feel sure I'm in bad form. Then I go to the start and do a good race. And sometimes I feel sure of winning or doing very well because I feel in top form and when I go off, I am in bad form. So warming up doesn't tell me anything.

Q: You also race in the 10,000 metres. That must be totally different?

A: Yes, different techniques and tactics. In this we are next to each other and using each other's waves. It's like bicycling. Then for the last 1000 metres we spread out and have to get into lanes. But it requires a lot of tactics. You get a lot of broken paddles and holes in boats! It's very exciting which is why I like this distance. Also because it's so different from the 500 or 1000.

Q: But that's like an athlete saying he's going to run the 400, 1500 and 10,000 metres. In athletics you couldn't do that, but in paddling you can. How do you explain that?

A: Well, the 1000 and the 10,000 aren't all that different. In the 10,000 it's so important to have speed to get into the correct position and the last 1000 metres is crucial. If we started at intervals of a minute then we could have 10,000 metre specialists but with the massed start you have to have so much speed that the same paddlers who are good in shorter distances are also good in the 10,000.

Q: So you don't train for just one of the three events? Your training is more general.

A: Yes, in the 1979 World Championships I came fifth in K1 over 500 metres, then first in K2 over 1000 and then second in K1 over 10,000. I do every race. But usually my speciality is the 1000 metres. That's the distance I'm thinking most about. But I enter every race because I think it's fun to race. I don't want to concentrate on one event, I want to do the lot because I love racing.

Andy Toro

Andy Toro (Hungary and USA) has been a distinguished paddler for the past twenty years. He represented Hungary at the 1960 and 1964 Olympic Games, then went to the 1968 and 1972 Games under the colours of the USA. He won a bronze medal in C2 in 1960 but now is a marathon enthusiast and thinks that this event has a greater future than the Olympic sprint events.

Q: Do you think flat water racing is rather dated? What do you think is going to take over from it?

A: I don't think it's getting out of date but I can see a trend towards marathon racing, using both kayaks and canoes.

Q: What is the attraction of marathon racing compared to flat water racing in the special basins used at international level?

A: Look at the economic situation. What is the point of building a 50 million dollar white elephant which is used maybe three or four times a year? It is just a big ditch, filled with water, and with athletes going back and forth on it. Compare this with marathon racing where you are on a beautiful scenic river. From start to finish you need only three or four people to organize the race, so when you start adding up all the costs, I think marathon racing is going to come out on top in future.

Q: But you took part in four Olympic Games in flat water racing. What's made you change your mind apart from the cost? Is there anything else about the appeal of marathon racing?

A: I think it's really the beauty of the sport. In canoeing you are closer to nature than in any other water sport. In flat water racing that element is taken out. Competitors aren't looking at nature but at some concrete wall or a bare gravel path and the beauty's not there any more. I hate to see that missing because I think it's an aspect of the sport we should preserve.

Q: What about the characteristics of the marathon canoeist or kayaker? What is he like compared with the sprinter?

A: If you get down to the basics, its pretty much the same but in marathon racing there are some natural elements which have to be overcome, like shallow water. Then of course there are the longer

97 Andy Toro in the bow of a Canadian canoe.

distances that have to be prepared for, so the mentality has to be different. Another thing to consider is that age really doesn't matter in marathon racing.

Q: You mean the youngsters don't have an advantage?

A: No, in my opinion the older you are, the better you are. It can be compared with marathon running; good marathon runners start developing between 27 and 32. I can see the very same thing in canoeing especially in the team boats when the rhythm and the power have to be maintained for hour after hour. I raced in four Olympic Games and I won a medal in 1960, then I won several medals in the United States as a marathon racer. It gives me great personal satisfaction that

I can keep going for 36 hours, paddling two nights in a row without sleeping. I accomplish more in life. I think you're going to be a better human being than when you do the 500-metre sprint, where you just blast out and one minute 45 seconds later you win the race. Of course, there is something about it that is appealing, but I think in comparison marathon racing will gain in popularity to the point when it is going to overtake flat water, Olympic-style sprint racing.

Q: You talk about racing for 36 hours. What sort of times and distances do you think are ideal for a marathon race?

A: Traditionally in the United States we go for very long distances. Twenty-five miles would be average. What we usually do is to combine marathon racing with sprint racing. At the end of the day we have a special section where there is a sort of 'victory loop' which is timed and whoever has the best time is awarded a sprint trophy. So it combines both sprint and marathon.

Q: What other differences are there between marathon racing in the United States and Canada and the other marathon countries like Australia, South Africa or European nations?

A: In the United States we do a lot more canoeing as opposed to kayaking. The C2 event is the most prestigious event and for the US National Championships 200 boats will show up. The mixed C2 with a man and a woman in the one canoe is also very popular, attracting between 60 and 100 boats in that particular class. The next class is called a touring C2 which is just a standard canoe. This compares with the K2 in Europe which is the most popular by far in all the European competitions. Then comes the K1. In my opinion the European system penalizes mixed events. It's discrimination.

Q: You're saying that in Europe, you have either men or women, but never mixed?

A: No, what I'm saying is that the canoeing event is cut in half because paddling an Olympic-type boat means you can't kneel for very long. I think we should change the boat. I'm confident that I could go out in a C2 against a K1 man in a 25-hour race and beat him. After about 12 hours I don't think any K1 paddler can stand up to a C2. They've proved that, over and over again in the United States. In the very confined K1 you can't move much, your legs go to sleep and your bottom goes out of shape. In a canoe you can do double kneeling, you can high kneel, you can sit; so changing positions every six hours you can go 60 to 65 hours easy. That's been proven. You can get all the food, all the provisions, in the boat. It's much easier to portage the boat and so I think there's a lot to be said for the C2. But the C boats are penalized under the European system because they still have to use the Olympic-type of canoe. You can't kneel more than about four hours even if you're really tough, so you have to reduce the race distance. Therefore — I suggest we change the boats. That is what I personally proposed to the ICF and that's the direction we're going in right now. The other thing is the women's events. With women's liberation in the United States they'd just kill anyone who wanted to shorten the distance so the women paddle the same distances as the men. They do very well; it's a medical fact that women athletes do well in the longer distances because they are more adapted physically. In the United States we are very conscious of that, so all the classes are open and race the same distance. Organizationally, this is much better.

Q: What about professional canoe racers? They seem to be prominent in the United States and Canada.

A: Traditionally it is very big in the United States. It started right after the war but even before that we had some professional racers up in Canada, in the Quebec area, and some in the United States. The two most prestigious events are the Au Sable in Michigan, which they have called the 'World Championships' for many, many years. It's a 17-hour non-stop race and the big class is obviously the men's C2. The purse for that is about 8000 dollars, with about 2500 dollars for the winner. The other big event is the International Canoe Classic, what the Canadians call the 'World Championships', up on the St Maurice River. That's a two-day event with about 6½ hours in the first day including the sprint race, and about 7 hours on the second day with another sprint race. The total purse up there is much bigger, getting to be around 20,000 dollars with all the sponsorship. So you can do pretty well. There are some smaller events in the United States, mainly in Michigan and Minnesota, and in Canada around Quebec and Toronto.

Q: What's the difference between a professional and an amateur marathon racer? Are there different tests or different conditions?

A: No, there is no difference so far as technique or preparation are concerned, but the boats are different. Their length is the same, but the amateurs use the so-called '4 x 32' which is a boat measured on a 4-inch water line where it has to be 32 inches wide. The professional boat is a '3 x 27' which, on a 3-inch water line has to be 27 inches wide, a narrower and sleeker boat and in theory faster. However, in some river conditions '4 x 32' does better than a '3 x 27', for instance, in rapids where stability is needed, or in shallows where you need a flat-bottomed boat. You always have to look at the state of the river and what kind of boat you're using.

Q: The appeal of a professional sport is that people pay to turn up and watch. Do spectators contribute enough to pay for all these prizes, or do the sponsors think they are doing a good turn for professional canoeists?

A: Some of the sponsors contribute money to local events and some are on television in Canada, though not in the United States yet.

Q: What do people see on television in an event where competitors are spread out over miles and miles and miles?

A: The start, the portages and the sprint finishes. Television can compress the whole race into ten minutes, using the most exciting parts.

Q: What sort of portages are they?

A: In the International Canoe Classic you have a 1-mile portage and it's very tough to have to pick up your canoe with your partner and run a mile after you have been paddling for about 4 hours. Some people can't even stand up! There's a lot happening there, so a portage is always the most exciting part of the race.

Q: Have you had a lot of top amateurs going through to the professional ranks? Is it a hindrance to the growth of amateur marathon racing?

A: Interestingly enough, no. For a while I thought it would happen but a lot of amateurs want to stay amateur. The money doesn't appeal to them that much. A lot of marathon amateurs do flat water racing as well, so they want to maintain their amateur status, although the US Olympic Committee as well as the ACA (American Canoe Association) have opened up the amateur rules now so the Association collects the money on the pro race. It's harder now for the professionals because the amateurs arrive at some of the races in very good physical condition and so they're always up in the top three or four. It's great for them because that's the way they earn money for a summer's racing, since the club gets money from the ACA and it's all perfectly legal.

APPENDIX
International Canoe Federation –Affiliated Members

Argentina Federacion Argentina de Canoas, Florida 229, 3°piso – of. 332, Buenos Aires.

Australia Australian Canoe Association, c/o P.J. Thompson, 30 Melaleca, Carrum 3197, Melbourne.

Austria Osterreichischischer Kanu-Verband, Bergganse 16, 1090 Wien. Tel. (0222) 349203. Cable: OE-Kanu Wien.

Belgium Federation Belge de Canoe, Belgisch Kano Verbond, c/o A. Vandeput, Geerdengemwaart 79, B. 2800, Mechelen. Tel. (015) 415459.

Bulgaria Bulgarian Canoe Federation, Bulevar Tolboukine 18, Sofia. Cable: Besefese-Sofia. Tel. 8651. Telex 22723-22723.

Canada Canadian Canoe Association, 333 River Road, Place Vanier, Vanier City, Ontario K1L 8B9. Tel. (613) 746-0060. Telex 053-3660.

Cyprus Cyprus Canoe Association, P.O. Box 1384, Nicosia.

Cuba Federation Cubana de Canotaje, c/o Comite Olimpico Cubano, Hotel Habana Libre, La Habana.

Czechoslovakia Czechoslovak Canoe Federation, Na porici 12, 11530 Praha 1. Cable: Sportsvaz-Praha. Tel. 249541-9. Telex cstv c 122650.

DPR of Korea Canoe Association of the Democratic People's, Moosing-Dong, Dongdawon District, Pyongyang.

Denmark Dansk Kano og Kajak Forbund, c/o J. Cronberg, Engvej 184-2300 Copenhagen S. Cable: Dancasport Copenhagen. Tel. (01) 554509.

Federal Republic of Germany Deutscher Kanu-Verband, Berta-Allee 8, 4100 Duisburg 1. Tel. (0203) 72965/72966.

Finland Suomen Kanoottiliitto ry, Topeliuksenkatu 41a, 00250 Helsinki 25.

France Federation Francaise de Canoe-Kayak, 87 Quai de la Marne, 94, 340 Joinville Le Pont. Tel. 873.79.25.

German Democratic Republic Deutscher Kanu-Sport-Verband. Storkowerstr. 118, 1055 Berlin. Cable: DTSB (Kanusport) Berlin. Tel. 4384342/4384396.

Great Britain British Canoe Union, Flexel House, 45/47 High Street, Addlestone, Weybridge, Surrey, KT15 1JV. Tel. Weybridge (97) 41341.

Hong Kong Hong Kong Canoe Union, Room 502, Mau Wai Commercial Building, 102 Wellington Street, Central Hong Kong.

Hungary Magyar Kajak-Kanu Szovetseg, Rosenberg Hazuspar u. 1, Budapest V. Cable: Comsport Kayak-Budapest. Tel. 114.800.

Iran Iranian Rowing and Water Ski Federation, Kakh Varzesh str. P.O. Box 3396, Teheran.

Ireland Irish Canoe Union, c/o Cospoir The National Sport Council, Floor 11, Hawkins House, Hawkins Street, Dublin 2.

Israel Israel Canoe Association, 8 Haarbaa Street, P.O.B. 7170, Tel-Aviv. Tel. 2601815.

Italy Commissione Italiana Canoa, Viale Tiziano 70, 00100 Roma. Tel. 36851.

Ivory Coast Ivory Coast Canoes and Pirogue Federation, B.P. 1872, Abidjan.

Japan Japan Canoe Association, c/o Kishi Memorial 1 – 1 – 1 Jinnan Shibuya-ku, Tokyo. Cable: JAAA Tokyo 'Kanoe.' Tel. 03-467-6794.

Luxembourg Federation Luxembourgeoise de Canoe-Kayak, Boite postale 424, Luxembourg 2. Tel. 29155.

Mexico Federation Mexicana de Canotaje, Sanchez Ascona 1348, Mexico 12, D.F. Tel. 575. 15.60/575. 13. 65.

Netherlands Nederlandse Kano Bond, Central Bureau, N. B., Henri Dunanstraat 62, 1561 Bd Krommenie.

New Zealand New Zealand Canoeing Association Inc., P.O. Box 5125, Auckland.

Norway Norges Kajak-Forbund, Hauger Skolovei 1, N. 1346 Gjettum.

People's Republic of China Canoeing Association of the People's Republic of China, 9 Tiyukuan Road, Peking. Cable: Sportschine Peking.

Poland Polski Zwiszek Kajakowy, ul. Sienkiewicza 12, 00-010 Warszawa. Cable: Kajak-Warszawa. Tel. 27.49.16.

Romania Federatia Romana de Caiac-Canoe, Str. Vasile Conta 16, 70139 Bucarest. Tel. 119787. Telex 11180. Cable: Sportrom-Bucarest.

Soviet Union Canoe Federation of the USSR, Skaternyi pereoulok 4, Moscow 69. Cable: Sportkomitet Moscow. Tel 2903940.

Spain Federcion Espagnola de Piraguismo, c/o Miguel Angel, num. 18,6° Madrid 10. Tel. 4103815/ 4104048.

Sweden Svenska Kanotforbundet, Idrottens Hus, 123 87 Farsta. Tel. 08-930500.

Switzerland Schweizerischer Kanu-Varband, c/o Frau G. Vogler-Lintner, Brunigstrasse 121, 6060 Sarnen. Tel. 041 66.34.88.

USA American Canoe Association, National Office, P.O. Box 242, Lorton, Virginia 22079.

Yugoslavia Kajakaski Savez Jugoslavije, Bulevar Revolucije 44/I, 11000 Beograd. Cable: Kajak Beograd.

South Africa South African Canoe Association, c/o W.F. van Riet, 13 Leopold Street, Bellville. (Suspended by the 1970 Congress in Copenhagen.)

GLOSSARY

ABEAM	at right angles to the centreline of the boat.
ABS	construction material (used for vacuum moulding).
AFT	towards the rear of the boat.
AHEAD	ahead of the canoe.
AIR BAGS	(see BUOYANCY)
ALL-IN RESCUE	the most difficult rescue, as all canoeists are in the water and start by rescuing the weakest man.
AMIDSHIPS	the central part of the canoe.
AMPLITUDE	the height of a wave, measured from the top of its crest, to the bottom of the trough.
ANORAK	light, lined, windproof jacket.
APRON	another word for spray cover
ASTERN	behind the canoe.
ASYMMETRICAL BLADE	racing blade, kidney-shaped, cut at an angle.
BACK PADDLING	reverse paddling to move backwards or to stop.
BACK STRAP	strap across back of bucket seat supporting paddler's lower back — particularly used in white water.
BAIDARKA	Russian name for Eskimo kayak of the Alentian Islands.
BALANCING REFLEX	maintaining balance by moving body rather than using leg-work.
BAT	initials of Baths Advanced Trainer used by learners for rolling, also for canoe polo.
BATH TRAINER	(see BAT)
BAT POLO	(see CANOE POLO)
BEAM	width of boat at its widest part.
BEAM SEA	when waves come from the side.
BILGE	the part inside the canoe below the waterline.
BIRCH-BARK CANOE	built by North American Indians; birch-bark covers a wooden frame.
BLACK WATER	opposite to white water — deep, safe water with no air bubbles.
BLADE	the broad end of the paddle that goes into the water.
BLOCKED WILD WATER	wild water containing lots of boulders.
BLOW-MOULDED	process of moulding plastics, which are first treated, then blown with air (used for ABS).
BLOWN OUT	when conditions are too bad for surfing due to strong winds.
BOIL	underwater current that comes to surface, creating inconsistent bubbling effect.
BOTTOM BOARD	slots into bottom of boat to take the canoeist's weight.
BOTTOM FEEL	(see FEEL BOTTOM)
BOTTOM TURN	a surfing turn made below the crest of a wave.
BOW	the front end of a canoe or kayak.
BOW AND STERN DIPPING	a canoe slalom technique devised to dip boat underneath gates.
BOW CARRY	used to rescue tired or panicky swimmer who simply hangs on to bow and is paddled ashore.
BOW DRAW STROKE	Canadian canoe stroke for minor changes of direction.

BOWMAN	paddler nearest bow.
BOW RESCUE	used for capsized paddler who cannot right himself by rolling and needs to hold on to a rescuer's bow.
BOW RUDDER	stroke to turn canoe's bow towards side on which bowman is paddling.
BOW SWEEP	used to turn a boat.
BOX	a series of waves that are bigger than usual.
BRACE	a recovery stroke, using the blade of the paddle, to prevent capsize.
BREAKER	wave in sea which breaks in shallow water.
BREAK-IN	a stroke forcing a canoe into the mainstream of current.
BREAK LINE	in sea, where the waves begin to break.
BREAK-OUT	a stroke forcing a canoe out of the mainstream.
BROACH	laying beam to the waves.
BROKEN WATER	usually refers to small rapid water that is not flat, e.g. broken by rapid.
BULKHEAD	rigid, airtight plate which prevents water entering forward or back part of boat.
BUOYANCY	sealed lightweight containers, expanded polystyrene or polyether foam wedged into bow and stern of a kayak to help it float.
BUOYANCY AIDS	used by competitors; close-fitting protective waistcoat which brings paddlers to surface of water.
BURN	a short sprint used in flatwater racing to try and drop other paddlers.
C1, C2, C4, etc.	class of competitive Canadian canoes: C denotes Canoe, the figure denotes number of paddlers.
CAGJAK	usually called 'cag' or 'cagoule' — similar to anorak — waterproof but unlined.
CAGOULE	(see CAGJAK above)
CANADIAN CANOE	based on the North American birch-bark canoe, propelled by single-blade paddle; sprint canoes are open; slalom and wild water have decks.
CANADIAN SLALOM CANOE	almost indistinguishable from, though wider, than kayak.
CANADIAN PADDLE	paddle with single blade.
CANOE	in Britain a collective term for canoes and kayaks; specifically, a long, pointed craft propelled by single-bladed paddle.
CANOE POLO	a version of water polo where contestants sit in kayaks and try to score goals, using their hands or paddles to shoot the ball.
CANOE SLALOM	a competition on fast flowing water where both obstacles and hanging 'gates' provide a test of manoeuvrability on two timed runs.
CANOE SURFING	a version of board surfing using kayaks; tricks can also be performed.
CANYON	a very deep gorge or ravine.
CAPSIZE DRILL	all beginners must master the skill of capsizing and then getting out of their boats while underwater.
CATARACT	very heavy rapid, usually in very broad river.
CATCHMENT AREA	area that drains into a river or larger expanse of water, e.g. lake or loch.
CATHERINE WHEEL	in surfing, a technique to spin the kayak through 360° while hurtling along a wave.
CHART	a map of the sea, and sea bed.
CHUTE	a narrow but clear route through weir or rapids.
CLAPOTIS	outgoing waves rebounding off walls or rocks clashing with incoming waves — dangerous.
CLIMBING AND DROPPING	in surfing, gliding up and down the face of a wave.
CLOSE-OUT	in surfing, a wave that breaks all along its length simultaneously, impossible to ride.

CLUB FOUR	American nickname for 20-foot V-bottom racing canoe, with 30-inch beam, used by four men.
COAMING	the raised edge of the cockpit to which a spray cover is attached.
COCKPIT	where paddler sits in a decked canoe or kayak.
COLD-MOULDED VENEER	old-fashioned, slow method of building kayak in wood.
COLORADO HOOK	old-fashioned paddling technique; right-hand blade put on left side of boat — leads to capsize.
COMPASS	used by canoeists, let into well in deck or carried on cord round neck.
CRASH HAT or HELMET	a must for most canoeists, it should have holes in it to let water out.
CREST	top of a wave.
CROSS BOW STROKE	similar to Colorado Hook but in C1 or C2.
CROSS SECTION	view of craft, like a slice from one side of beam to the other.
CSM	(chopped strand mat) glassfibre construction material.
CURE	a construction term; GRP needs time to set or dry out properly; often 2-3 weeks.
CURL	top of wave that is just breaking.
CUT AWAY	in surfing, after a run the craft is turned over a wave before it breaks.
CUT BACK	in surfing, turning back towards the shoulder of a wave.
CUTTING OUT	turning fast moving canoe into an eddy. (Another term for break-out.)
DECK	the top cover of a kayak, or closed canoe; may also refer to spray deck or apron.
DECK LINES	thin ropes running round decks of sea canoes, used to lash equipment to or for rescue.
DEEP WATER RESCUE	techniques used in rough, open sea.
DIOLEN	modern polyester material used to reinforce canoes and kayaks.
DIP	point where paddle enters water on stroke (US).
DIVE AND SPIN OUT	surfing term.
DOUBLE BLADE	used by kayakers; a paddle with blades at both ends.
DOUBLE END FORM	cross-section of canoe that is symmetrical.
DOUBLE PADDLE	(see DOUBLE BLADE)
DOUBLE TOURING	2-seat kayak used for touring.
DOWN RIVER RACING	race down a river — paddler chooses the course and fastest time wins.
DRAW STROKE	used to move boat sideways.
DRIFT	when boat is moved sideways by current or wind.
DRIP RINGS	rubber or plastic rings fitted near blades of double paddles to stop water running down loom on to paddler's hands.
DROP IN	in surfing, spoiling another surfer's ride by getting in his way.
DROP OFF	surfing term for coming off a wave.
DRY LOOP	a surfing trick where paddler somersaults and turns without getting wet.
DRYSUIT	a loose watertight garment that fits closely at neck, ankles and wrists.
DUFFEK	hanging stroke named after its Czech inventor, used to turn kayak at speed.
DULUTH PACK	a canvas bag for carrying food.
DUMPER	in surfing, waves that are too steep to ride.
EDDY	swirling water that flows upstream as current bounces off banks, rocks, etc.
END LOOPS	loop of cord fixed at bow and stern for lifting or tying up craft.
EROSION	where soil is worn away by wind or water.
ESKIMO KAYAK	used for hunting, this long, thin craft is completely decked in, and is the forerunner of today's sea kayak.

ESKIMO RESCUE	(see BOW RESCUE and SIDE RESCUE)
ESKIMO ROLL	Eskimo technique adopted by modern kayakers to right craft without getting out of it, turning a full 360°.
ESPADA	popular make of inexpensive K1 in Britain.
FACE	in paddle racing, concave side of paddle blade. In surfing, the smooth front of a wave.
FACE REVERSE PIROUETTE	in surfing, a trick move.
FACE ROLL	in surfing, a manoeuvre based on the Eskimo roll.
FEATHER	to turn a blade at 90° as it leaves the water; prevents water being lifted out by paddle — cuts down wind resistance.
FEEL BOTTOM	a wave feels bottom just before it breaks in shallow water.
FERRULE	of brass, around centre of old touring paddles.
FERRY GLIDE	a technique for crossing a stream at an angle, so that current propels boat sideways towards the bank.
FETCH	the effect of wind on the sea, driving waves in one direction.
FINAL STABILITY	describes canoe's resistance to capsizing when on its side.
FISH FORM	kayak hull whose waterline is wider in front of cockpit than behind it.
FLAT WATER	water without rapids; used for sprint canoeing when competitors usually race in lanes.
FLARE	distress signal that gives off bright light and sometimes loud bang.
FLICK AND PIROUETTE	a surfing move.
FLOORBOARD	used in bottom of wood or canvas boats.
FOAM CORE CONSTRUCTION	high density polyurethane with a GRP skin is used in surf skis.
FOLLOWING SEA	waves that come from behind, throwing the paddler forward.
FOOT REST	made of wood, alloy or fibreglass; by pushing the feet against it, paddler gets better grip on craft.
FORWARD	towards the bow.
FORWARD LOOP	in surf canoeing — a forward somersault.
FORWARD SWEEP STROKE	paddle put in near bow, then swept in wide arc away from side of boat.
FREEBOARD	the area between the waterline and the gunwale.
FREE GATE	marked with black and white rings, this is a slalom gate that can be taken in any direction.
FREQUENCY	the time between one wave crest and the next passing a fixed point.
GATE	used in the slalom. These gates are made of two poles hanging above the water. Paddlers must pass between the poles (port marked red/white, starboard green/white) without touching them.
GEL COAT	elastic polyester resin which is the outside layer of moulded boat.
GLACIAL STREAM	fed by water from melting glacier, at its lightest in summer.
GORGE	formed by river cutting deep between steep banks.
GRADES OF DIFFICULTY	used to indicate degree of difficulty of rivers, ranging from I (suitable for beginners) to VI for experts only.
GRAVE YARD	rapid with a lot of rocks showing above water.
GREEN WAVES	unbroken; before the white water.
GRP	glass reinforced plastic, used to build most modern canoes.
GUNWALE/GUNNEL	the top edge of the hull, where it joins the deck.
HANDROLL	a most difficult way of rolling using the hand only, as paddle.
HANGING SUPPORT STROKE	(see DUFFEK strokes)
HAYSTACK	a standing wave, topped with white water.
HEAD/SEA	waves coming head on; easier to handle than they appear.

132

HIGH CROSS	fast ferry glide using high paddle stroke.
HIGH WATER	when tide is at its highest on beach or when river is full to flooding.
HIP BOARDS	join bucket seat to cockpit rim — in the cockpit prevent slalom paddler from sliding from side to side.
HIP FLICK	rotation of hips used to right an overturned kayak.
HI RESCUE	also known as the Ipswich Rescue.
HOG	the strengthener running down the centre of the hull on the inside.
HOLDING COURSE	boat's tendency to travel in right direction.
HOLLOW	face of paddle blade.
HOT MOULDED VENEER	expensive, professional way of building a kayak in wood — using sheets of veneer.
H-RESCUE	where rescue boats form sides of H to pick up capsized boat.
HULL	lower part of kayak or canoe that comes into direct contact with water.
HUMPER	in surfing, large, unbroken wave.
HUT!	canoeist's signal for changing sides when paddling open canoe.
HYDRAULIC JUMP	(see STOPPER)
HYPOTHERMIA	severe loss of body heat, usually associated with exhaustion and accelerated by wet. Women are less susceptible than men; older men less than youngsters; short, thick-set youngsters less than tall, thin ones.
IC CLASS	the International Canoe sailing class, the fastest single hull in the world.
ICF	initials of the International Canoe Federation, the governing body of the sport, founded in 1946.
INITIAL STABILITY	describes canoe's resistance to capsizing when upright.
INJECTION MOULDED CONSTRUCTION	steel moulds clamped together and injected with heated, melted plastic which covers the surface.
INSIDE	in surfing, the area between the breakline and the beach.
IPSWICH RESCUE	(see HI RESCUE)
IRK	the first governing body of the sport founded in 1924 — Internationalen Repraesentation Kanusport.
J STROKE	Canadian paddle stroke, tracing a J in the water. The end of the stroke helps to steer the canoe.
K1, K2, K4, etc.	classes of competitive kayak: K denotes kayak, the figure denotes number of paddlers.
KAYAK	today's version of the Eskimo kayak is also propelled with a two-bladed paddle.
KEELSON	an internal strengthening running the length of the canoe keel.
KEELSTRIP	strip of wood down outside of a hull which protects keel.
KETTLE HOLE	foaming water behind rock.
KEVLAR	aromatic polyanide used for canvas.
KLEPPER	manufacturers of the unsinkable Arius kayak.
KNEE BRACE	wooden bar or indentations (underneath cockpit rim) for thighs or knees to push/pull against.
KNEE GRIPS	same as knee brace.
LABYRINTH	where canoeist cannot see clear route ahead between boulders.
LAMINATE	construction technique using thin layers of wood, fibreglass, etc. bonded with resin.
LDR	initials for Long Distance Racing — see MARATHON.
LEANING	deliberately tilting the boat over.
LEEBOARDS	boards used on sailing canoes to prevent drift.

LEEWARD	side of craft away from wind.
LEFT RUN	in surfing, when a surfer rides to his left.
LEG WORK	used by kayakers to manoeuvre their craft.
LIE OUT	paddler supports himself on the water by laying paddle blade flat on surface and sculling for support.
LIFEDECK	a combined buoyancy aid and spray deck.
LIFE JACKET	open-backed jacket which will bring a paddler to surface of water face up.
LINE UP	in surfing, where participants want to catch a wave.
LINE DOWN	floating canoe down through rocky water, keeping hold of rope ('painter').
LOCKED IN	in surfing, when a surfer gets caught by a wave or when he rides a tube.
LOOM	the shaft of the paddle, joining the blades.
LOOP	surfing stunt; boat goes through 180° turn after bow dips down.
MACGREGOR, JOHN	the father of modern canoeing, built first canoe in Europe in 1865.
MAINSTREAM	where strongest, deepest flow of water lies.
MANOEUVRE	any turning movement of craft.
MARATHON	long distance races, usually at least 10 miles or two hours duration.
MEANDER	a very twisty river that tends to double back on itself.
MIRROR DESCENT	smooth water on a stream behind weirs, steps or rafting channels.
MODIFIED SWEDEN FORM	kayak hull that is at its widest amidships.
MOMENT OF INERTIA	Body's resistance to turning movement.
MOULD	shell which gives form to material injected into it.
MOUNTAIN STREAM	fed by water from lakes or springs, at its highest in spring or after rain.
MUSHROOM	currents that 'mushroom' upwards, breaking throught surface of water. (see BOIL)
NARROWS	where sea rushes between two islands, or the shore and an island. The result is turbulence.
NEAP TIDE	season of low high tides and high low tides, giving minimum contrast.
NEOPRENE	tough synthetic rubber used for spray covers and wetsuits.
NEW YORK CANOE CLUB	oldest canoe club in North America, founded 1871 by William Alden and M. Roosevelt Schnyler.
NOSE DIVING	in surfing, kayak plunges bow first into sand.
OBJECTIVE DANGER	danger presented by environment.
OPEN WATER	a river estuary on the sea.
OUTBOARD MOTOR	used to propel canoes in North America.
OUTRIGGER	second hull or paddle used to stabilize craft.
OUTSIDE	in surfing, the area of open sea beyond the breakline.
OVERFALL	a submerged reef in the sea that causes currents to boil up to the surface.
PADDLE	used to propel boats; canoe paddles have one blade; kayak paddles have two blades.
PADDLE BRACE	overhead stroke used at speed; paddle pulled towards craft.
PADDLE HOLD	(see PADDLE PARK)
PADDLE PARK	loop or loops in deckline used for holding paddle.
PADDLE RACING	(see SPRINT)
PADDLER	familiar name for canoeist or kayaker.
PADDLE SUPPORT	using paddle to prevent capsize.
PAINTER	a rope tied to the bow or stern.

PAWLATA	the man credited with bringing the Eskimo roll to Europe; his version of it keeps the paddler leaning forward throughout.
PEAK	the highest point of a wave.
PEANUT	American nickname of V-bottom cedar racing canoe; 16 foot long, 30-inch beam, now outdated by Olympic C1.
PEARL DIVE	in surfing. (see NOSE DIVE)
PIROUETTE	in surfing, a vertical spin in a kayak.
PLANING	when boat travels at such speed that hull actually comes out of water.
PLUG	form from which mould is made.
PLYWOOD CONSTRUCTION	can be light; fairly durable; needs maintenance.
POINT	land sticking out into sea.
POINT BREAKS	where point breaks up waves and sets up good surfing conditions.
POLE VAULTING	in surfing, when bow of kayak hits sand when trying to loop.
POLING	in North America, the tradition of poling a canoe, rather than paddling it, is still maintained.
POLYETHER FOAM	construction material.
POP OUT	(see SKY ROCKET)
PORT, PORTSIDE	the left-hand side (looking forward).
PORTAGE	from the French, meaning to carry boats round an obstacle, from water to water.
POT HOLE	where riverbed is hollowed out behind waterfalls, steps or weirs.
PRY-OVER	a Canadian canoe stroke, used to move craft sideways.
PULL	part of paddle stroke when blade is in the water.
PULL OUT	in surfing, refers to the end of a run when surfer pulls out over a wave to paddle back out.
PURL	when kayak buries its nose in the water.
PUT ACROSS	method of rolling — with blade at 90° angle to boat; upside down paddler pulls against paddle to bring body upright.
QUARTER DECK	rear part of deck.
RACING CANOE	used on flat water, it has little super-structure and little stability.
RACING KAYAK	used on flat water, designed for speed and has little stability.
RACING PADDLE	designed with hollow-faced blades, very rigid shaft.
RAFTING UP	using paddles to bind several craft together in rows to form a raft.
RAIL	in surfing, the gunwale.
RAPIDS	foaming water due to water running across main current and over rocks or uneven riverbed.
RAVINE	where water flows between steep walls of rock.
RECOVERY	either the time between paddling strokes or a stroke used in the Eskimo roll to right boat.
REEF	underwater barrier that makes waves break.
RE-ENTRY	in surfing, more difficult than a plain cut-back, when canoe bounces off the curl of the wave.
REFLECTED WATER	where water bounces back off reflection slope and breaks surface.
REFLECTION SLOPE	the bank outside of a bend in a river.
RESCUE LOOPS	(see END LOOPS)
RESIN	material used to reinforce fibreglass, kevlar, diolen.
REVERSE LOOPS	in surfing, a backward somersault in a kayak.
REVERSE SCREW ROLL	screw roll performed leaning backwards.
REVERSE SWEEP STROKE	sweep stroke from stern, turning back away from stern.

RIB	strengthening on boat frame, running from keel to gunwale in wooden craft — in modern boats ribs run gunwale to gunwale to strengthen deck.
RIFFLE	section of fast flowing river with lots of waves but no stoppers.
RIGHT RUN	in surfing, when a surfer rides to his right.
RIP	(see TIDE RIP)
RIVER GUIDE	a map of a river, marking obstacles and other difficulties.
RIVER RACING	(see WHITE WATER)
ROB ROY	the original clinker-built canoes designed by John MacGregor in 1865; until 1900 the term was used generally for any kayak in Britain.
ROCKER	the curved banana-like shape of the keel of a kayak.
ROLL	any means of righting a kayak that has overturned.
ROLLER COASTING	in surfing, running up and down the shoulder of a wave.
ROYAL CANOE CLUB	the world's oldest canoe club, founded in 1866 by John MacGregor, near London, England.
RP	reinforced plastic — the most widely used construction material.
RUDDER	used to steer kayaks; can be 'over-stern' or 'under-stern'.
RUNNING BACKWARDS	in surfing, straightforward ride backwards.
RUNNING FORWARDS	in surfing, simple ride.
RUN-OFF	extra water in river due to rain or thaw.
SAILING CANOE	(see IC CLASS)
SAND LOOP	(see POLE VAULTING)
S-TURN	a break-in followed by a break-out to cross stream.
SCREW ROLL	an Eskimo roll executed with hands in the normal paddling position.
SCULLING DRAW	a stroke used to keep moving the boat sideways.
SCULLING FOR SUPPORT	stroke used to stop boat capsizing.
SEA KAYAK	specially designed craft for sea trips; often very long with sharp nose, extra deck lines, bulkheads, pumps, etc.
SEAL LANDING, LAUNCH	used when a paddler lands or launches himself when still in boat, using wave to carry him.
SEAL SUIT	type of wetsuit.
SET	(see BOX)
SHAFT	(see LOOM)
SHEER	the convex or concave shape of gunwale — referred to as positive or negative sheer.
SHEETING	wood strips nailed to the ribs to provide a craft's strength; to protect outside of wood or wood and canvas.
SHOOT	to go down a rapid.
SHOOT THE TUBE/CURL	in surfing, riding high on the wave in the 'tube' caused as wave breaks.
SHOREBREAK	in surfing, dumpers unsuitable for riding.
SHOULDER	in surfing, the unbroken part of the wave, just in front of the curl.
SIDE RESCUE	used for capsized paddler who cannot right himself by rolling; rescuer puts himself parallel to upturned boat and capsized paddler hauls himself up on paddle.
SINGLE BLADE	(see SINGLE PADDLE)
SINGLE PADDLE	the Canadian canoe paddle, with T-shaped handle.
SKEG	a fixed rudder for kayaks to help keep a straight line.
SKY ROCKET	in surfing, when kayak is thrown vertically into the air by force of waves.
SLACK WATER	when tide is having little influence and water is not moving much.
SLALOM	(see CANOE SLALOM)

SLALOM CANOES	must be highly manoeuvrable and so have highly rockered keels, banana-shaped.
SLALOM COURSES	usually 800 metres long, with special gates suspended from wires above fast-flowing river presenting a twisty course for the paddler.
SLALOM PADDLE	short paddle used for competition.
SLAP SUPPORT	using flat paddle blade as a support.
SLIDING SEAT	used in sailing canoe.
SLIP-OFF SLOPE	the bank on the inside of a bend in a river.
SLIPPING IN	guiding a canoe back into the mainstream.
SLOT	in surfing, the man 'in the slot' is riding in the right place on the shoulder.
SLUICE GATE	Opened and closed to control flow of water from, say, dam to river below. Dangerous for canoeists.
SNAG	obstacle in river.
SOUP	in surfing, the frothy water after a wave has broken.
SPATE	river in flood.
SPIN MOULDED	a construction method, involving spinning mould at high speed.
SPIN OUT	(see DIVE AND SPIN OUT)
SPOONED BLADE	with the face spooned out like a spoon the paddler gets more purchase on the water.
SPOUT	(see TONGUE)
SPRAY COVER/DECK	fixed to canoeist's waist and fitted snugly round cockpit coaming, it stops water getting into boat.
SPRING TIDES	season when high tides are very high, and low tides very low, giving maximum contrast.
SPRINT	competitive events over 500, 1000 and 10,000 metres on still, flat water. K1, K2, K4, C1, C2, C7 compete at international level.
STABILITY	canoe's resistance to capsizing.
STALL	in surfing, trying to slow the kayak down by pointing up a wave or leaning backwards.
STARBOARD	right-side of boat (looking forward).
STEM	bow of boat.
STEPS	either man-made or natural; can be used to descend river.
STERN	the rear end of a canoe or kayak.
STERN CARRY	rescue method where man in water holds on to stern.
STERN-MAN	paddler nearest stern.
STERN RUDDER STROKE	when paddle is held at side of boat and used as a stabilizer in surf or current.
STERN SWEEP	backwards bow sweep used to turn boat.
STEYR ROLL	a version of the Eskimo roll, where the paddler leans backwards throughout.
STILL WATER SLALOM	often used as practise for white water slalom; being promoted as competitive.
STIFFENER	used in construction of boats.
STOPPER	a vertical eddy, where water appears to flow upstream, it has a braking effect on canoe.
STORM ROLL	unusual version of Eskimo roll.
SUBJECTIVE DANGER	danger caused by canoeist's own error.
SUCTION	water contriving to pull boat down.
SUCTION EDDY	very dangerous whirlpool, often occurring in front of sluice gates.

SUPPORT	type of stroke, out of side.
SURF	long rolling waves that can support kayak or board.
SURF CANOE	specially designed flat-bottomed kayak for surfing.
SURF SHOE	(see SURF CANOE above)
SURF SKI	what it sounds like — a long, narrow craft.
SWEDEN/SWEDISH FORM	cross-section of kayak that is wider behind cockpit than in front of it.
SWEEP	a stroke used to turn the canoe.
SWEEP AND CLIMB	a surfing term.
SWEEP TURN	a turning stroke.
SWING OUT	surfing term.
SWITCHING	when two open canoe paddlers change sides.
SYMMETRICAL FORM	(see MODIFIED SWEDEN FORM)
TAKE OFF	in surfing, to start on a run.
TANDEM	a double canoe or kayak.
TELEMARK	a kayak stroke where the paddle is held out to one side and used as a pivot to turn on.
TENO-SYNOVITIS	soreness of the wrist caused by poor paddling technique.
THWARTS	cross strengtheners of open canoe.
TIDE	the rise and fall of sea level at any point, occurring twice a day.
TIDE EBB	when tide goes out.
TIDE FLOW	when tide comes in.
TIDE RACE	the fast flow of water, often through a narrow gap, as tide rises or falls.
TIDE RIP	(see TIDE RACE above)
TILLER BAR	foot control for rudder.
TIMBER RAFTING CHANNEL	special route past weirs used by loggers to float timber downstream; can be used by canoeists.
TINGLE	a patch to repair a hole or crack in a canoe or kayak.
TIP	end of paddle.
TOGGLE	end-loop on canoe.
TONGUE	indicates correct route to take on wild water; also called the V.
TOURING CANOE	for everyday use as opposed to competition.
TOURING PADDLE	usually long and narrow, therefore unsuitable for wild water sprinting.
TOW	pulling a canoe from the bank with ropes tied fore and aft.
TRANSIT	lining up two fixed objects, transits, to steer a course.
T-RESCUE	where rescue boat pulls capsized boat over its bow.
TRIM	either level at which a canoe or kayak rides in the water, the balance of a canoe or kayak.
TROUGH	the lowest part between the waves.
TUBE	in surfing, the hollow formed as a wave curls over forming a tube.
TUMBLEHOME	the amount by which the craft curves in from the maximum width of the gunwale.
TUMPLINE	a leather strap for securing a food container. (see WANNIGAN)
TURNING MOMENT	force required to turn a canoe on the spot.
TWO SEATER	canoe or kayak for two paddlers.
UMIAK	large open craft used by Eskimos for caarrying gear or for trading.
UNDERCUT	when current pulls paddle or deck down.
UNDERTOW	current below surface moving in opposite direction to main current.
UNDERWATER SLUICE GATE	a dangerous gadget as it attracts suction eddies.
WAKE RIDING	(see WASH-HANGING)

WALTZING	technique for crossing river sideways.
WANNIGAN	North American Indian term for a wooden box for carrying food in canoes.
WAR CANOE	large open canoe, popular in North America, paddled by some nine canoeists.
WASH BOARD	(see COAMING)
WASH-HANGING	sitting on bow wake of craft in front; tactic used in 10,000 metre and marathon races.
WATERLINE	where surface of water touches hull.
WAVELENGTH	the distance from one wave crest to the next.
WEIR	a man-made step in the river; deceptively dangerous.
WEIR SLOT	(see SHOOT)
WETSUIT	designed to keep paddler warm, made of neoprene.
WHIRLPOOL	eddy that can suck boat or paddler under.
WHITE WATER	where water foams over rocks, wild water.
WIGGLE TEST	for performance fitness; involves doing it in a number of different times.
WILD BED	river bed with irregular bottom.
WILD WATER RACING	a competition on fast-flowing water with man-made and natural obstacles. One timed run is allowed for C1, C2 and K1 competitions.
WILD WATER CANOE	designed to be fast with certain amount of rocker for manoeuvrability.
WINDAGE	height of canoe or kayak above water that provides wind resistance.
WINDWARD	the direction from which the wind is blowing.
WRIGGLE TEST	(see WIGGLE TEST)
YAW	canoe going off course by swinging from side to side.
YOKE	usual central thwart — either cross-piece in open Canadian canoe used for carrying it or cross-piece on a rudder to which control lines are attached.

INDEX

(Figures in brackets indicate illustrations)

Berg Race, The 120
Bishop, Nathaniel H. 11
Blue Water Classic 120
British Canoe Union 105

Camping Club of Great Britain 12
Canoes
    construction and design of 13, 18-20, (19)
    correct size for paddler 23
    handling of 39, 40, (40)
    history of 9-12
    paddling strokes 35-37
    types of 13-16
Canoe polo 105, (106), 107-110
Canoe sailing 109-111, (110-111)
Care and maintentance 35-48
Clothing 42, (42)
Coaching 96-99
Cock, Oliver 105
Competitions, types of
    sprint 75-82, (75-81)
    slalom 82-86, (82), (84-86)
    wild water 86-91, (90)
    marathon 91-95, (92-94)

Devizes to Westminster Race 115, 116
Drown proofing (see Safety)

Eskimo roll 10, 52

First aid
    hypothermia 54
    warming 55
    asphyxia 55
Fitness
    physical types 61-63
    exercises 63, 64, 67, (71)
    anaerobic training 65
    motivation sheets 66, (66/67)
    weight training 67, 68, (68), (71)
    diet 69, 70
    isometric training 70, (72), 73, (73)
Fox, Richard (27)

Gudena Race 65, 69, 97, 115, (119), 119

Hedge, Alan (85)

Ice-Breaker Race 120
International Canoe Classic 119, 120
International Canoe Federation (ICF) 12, 127, 128
Internationaler Reprasentation fur Kanoesport
   (IRK) 11

Kayaks
    construction and design of 13, 18-20
    correct size for paddler 23
    foot rests 22
    handling of 40, 41, (41)
    history of 9-12
    paddling strokes 29-34, (29-34)
    rudders for 22, (22)
    types of 16-18, (16-18)
Kerr, Albert (41), (85)

Liffey Race 120

MacGregor, John 10, (10), 11
MacKenzie, Alexander 112
Mackereth, Graham 39, 41
Marquette, Jacques 112
Midwood, Pete (101)

New York Canoe Club 11
North American canoeing 111-114, (113)

Paddle blades 20, 21, (21)
Paddle handles 20, 21, (21)
Pawlata, H.W. 11, 12, 52, 53
Pawlata roll 52-54
Peterborough Co. of Canada 14
Planning a trip 44, 45
Pontevedra Race 119
Pope, Geoffrey 12

Rasmussen 12
Rasmussen, Einar (121), 120-123
Rescues, forms of 57-60
River guide, example of 43, 44, (44)
'Rob Roy' canoe 10, 11, (11), 14
Romer, Capt. Franz 12

Rules of the road   43

Safety
    points of safety   49
    personal   49
    boat   50
    survival   50, 51
    capsizing   51, (51)
    rolling   11, 52, 53, (53)
    rafting up   54
    drown proofing   55, 56, (56-58)
Saltin, Dr Bengt   69
Screw roll   53
Sea canoeing   100-102, (101)
Seidel, Erik   12
Sella Race   116, (116), 117, 118
Spray covers   21, 22, (22), 50, (50)

Spray decks   21, 22, 50
Spray sheets   21, 22, 50
Surf canoeing   102, 103, (103), 104, (104)
Surf ski   17, (18)

Taylor, Sheldon   12
Toro, Andy   123-126, (124)

Umiak   9

Wain, Nicy   (85)
Water
    techniques in   26-37
    understanding of   24-26
    formation of rapids   25, (25)
    stoppers   25, (25), 26